Pension Fund
Administration

Pension Fund Administration

edited by
A. G. Shepherd, LL B, FCIS, FCIArb, FPMI

ICSA Publishing · Cambridge

ICSA Publishing Limited
Fitzwilliam House
32 Trumpington Street
Cambridge CB2 1QY

First published 1984

© ICSA Publishing Limited 1984

ISBN 0 902197 15 0

Text design by Geoff Green

Phototypeset by Wyvern Typesetting Limited, Bristol

Printed in Great Britain by St Edmundsbury Press,
Bury St Edmunds, Suffolk

Foreword

by John F. Phillips, CBE, LL M, QC, FCIS

Past President and formerly Secretary and Chief Executive,
Institute of Chartered Secretaries and Administrators

I am delighted to have the opportunity, at the invitation of Mr A. G. Shepherd, of writing a foreword to this new and important volume published by ICSA Publishing. In particular, I should like to offer congratulations to the Council and Secretary of the Institute of Chartered Secretaries and Administrators for the high quality and standard of service not only to members but also to professional administrators and advisers, provided by this work on pension fund administration.

In view of the great and increasing importance of pensions, not only in our business lives but also in our social and economic circumstances as individuals, it was very timely to commission this study and to secure in its completion the active support of the Institute's Pension Administrators' Panel and the help of so many experienced practitioners in the various professions involved in pensions administration.

From my own experience in pension matters in various organisations, commercial and charitable, in both the public and private sectors, I have no hesitation in commending this comprehensive yet eminently readable review of 'best practice' in pensions administration, which I am confident will command an enthusiastic welcome and a wide readership, not only from members – and students – of the Institute, but also from the wider world of professional administration in our economic life.

John F. Phillips

Contents

Preface

by A. G. Shepherd, LL B, FCIS, FCIArb, FPMI

Group Pensions Manager, Grand Metropolitan PLC, 1969–83; Past Treasurer and Member of Council, National Association of Pension Funds, 1975–83

When ICSA Publishing first asked if I would be willing to act as Editor for their proposed volume on pension fund administration, I was understandably somewhat reluctant, in view of the many other books on pension matters which already filled my shelves.

However, after further examination of the proposed subject matter by the Pension Administrators' Panel of the Institute, we came to the conclusion that while there were many books dealing with the specialised legal and technical matters relating to pension schemes, there was still an identifiable need for a modest-sized volume dealing with the practical side of pensions administration. We have therefore assembled such a work with the help of some of the leading administrators and professional experts in the pensions field.

The intention has been to provide a book which would be readily understandable by company secretaries and others who are not necessarily familiar with pension problems on a first-hand basis but who wish to have a better grasp of the workings of a pension department for which they may have administrative responsibility. It may also be of considerable use to students, and contains a great deal which will be useful to professional pension fund managers and their advisers.

We hope that this volume will be treated not so much as a work of reference, but rather as the complete story of the daily workings of a pension scheme. It includes most, but not necessarily all, of those matters which would fall to the responsibility of a full-time pensions manager.

My fellow contributors have asked that I should draw the attention of our readers to the hard fact that pensions legislation is once more on the move. While we have all endeavoured to present the situation as it is at the time of going to press, it is inevitable that by the time the book appears there may have been further developments on such familiar topics as the portability of personal pension arrangements, the mandatory escalation of deferred pensions, disclosure (especially in Annual Reports and Accounts of pension schemes) and the possible improvement of additional voluntary contribution facilities. Subject to that proviso, we have endeavoured to provide an assembled mix of all that is good practice in the United Kingdom at the time of going to press.

In conclusion, I should like to express my thanks to Barry Barker, the Secretary of the Institute of Chartered Secretaries and Administrators, for all the encouragement he has given, not merely to the writing of this book, but also to the members of the Pension Administrators' Panel who have been closely associated with the work. Peter Bullard and Ken Collins have made many helpful suggestions for the improvement of the text and general layout and Alan Chapman assisted with the preparation of the Glossary.

I should also wish to pay my own personal tribute to the many distinguished outside contributors without whose collaboration we should never have been able to reach the high standard for which we aimed. A full attribution list for those chapters where a single contributor has been solely responsible for the text is given opposite.

My successor as Group Pensions Manager at Grand Metropolitan PLC, Mike Coombe, has been very generous in providing much of the illustrative matter in the Appendixes. He also carried out the onerous task of proof reading. The manuscript was typed by Mrs Moira Shedden and Miss Kathy Fernandes whose ability to read my drafts deserved the highest admiration.

A. G. Shepherd

The contributors

John Bolton, OBE (Chapter 15)
Formerly Principal at the Department of Health and Social Security whose
responsibilities included occupational pension matters

Alan Chapman, FCIS, FPMI (Chapter 13)
Group Pensions Manager, Rank Xerox Ltd

Phil Cooke, FPMI (Chapter 14)
Director, Lowndes Associated Pensions Ltd

David Hager, MA, FIA (Chapter 11)
Bacon & Woodrow, Consulting Actuaries

Tom Heyes, BSc (Econ.) (Chapter 10)
Head of Investments Department, ICI PLC

John Prevett, OBE, FIA (Chapter 8)
Bacon & Woodrow, Consulting Actuaries

Ron Spill, BA, APMI (Chapter 5)
Controller, Pensions Marketing, Legal & General Assurance

Peter Styles, FPMI (Chapter 4)
Head of Pensions, F. W. Woolworth plc

Guide to statutory references

FA 1956   Finance Act 1956. Provided for self-employed pension arrangements. Replaced by ICTA 1970, s.226.

FA 1970   Finance Act 1970. Set out the requirements for new Code approval (Part II, Chapter II).

ICTA 1970   Income and Corporation Taxes Act 1970. Covered the funding of pensions for the self-employed (s.226).

SSA 1973   Social Security Act 1973. Required approved schemes to give equal access and provide compulsory preservation in case of early withdrawal.

SSPA 1975   Social Security Pensions Act 1975. Set out the conditions for contracting out of the new State earnings-related pension scheme for upper tier earnings.

FA 1981   Finance Act 1981. Under s.32 the purchase of individual deferred annuity policies from life offices of the member's choice was permitted as an alternative to a deferred paid-up scheme pension or to a transfer payment to another approved scheme.

Common abbreviations

ARP   Accrued Rights Premium
AVC   Additional Voluntary Contribution
CEP   Contributions Equivalent Premium
CGT   Capital Gains Tax
CPA   Compulsory Purchase Annuity
CTT   Capital Transfer Tax
ECON   Employer's Contracting Out Number
EPB   Equivalent Pension Benefit
ERP   Earnings-related Pension
GMP   Guaranteed Minimum Pension
LRP   Limited Revaluation Premium
MLI   Market Level Indicator
NAPF   National Association of Pension Funds
NRD   Normal Retirement Date
OPAS   Occupational Pensions Advisory Service
OPB   Occupational Pensions Board
PHI   Permanent Health Insurance
PLA   Purchased Life Annuity
PMI   Pensions Management Institute
PRAG   Pensions Research Accountants Group
PRP   Pensioner's Rights Premium
PUP   Paid-up Pension
RNI   Return of contributions with no interest
RPI   Retail Price Index
RWI   Return of contributions with interest
SCON   Scheme Contracted Out Number

SFO	Superannuation Funds Office
SPA	State Pensionable Age
WGMP	Widow's Guaranteed Minimum Pension

1 Starting a pension scheme

The problems involved in starting a pension scheme may appear an academic exercise to many of our readers and not one which they will have to face in practice. But mergers and takeovers still occur with unfailing regularity and so we have endeavoured to set out the basic processes involved and to indicate the *best practice* wherever that is appropriate. We trust that this chapter will also help readers to set a bench-mark on what is actually happening in their own schemes.

This chapter will cover the following:
(1) The *ab initio* situation when setting up a new pension scheme for a new company and new staff without any existing pension arrangements.
(2) The situation where existing pension arrangements are being wound up in a merger and completely new pension arrangements are being started for all employees.

Basically both situations carry the same fundamental problems, except in the case of (2) where past service rights from service in the closed scheme will be involved and special arrangements are necessary.

The position of the existing members of a closed scheme who have been taken over by a new employer company is dealt with in Chapter 9. *Best practice* is to avoid running two parallel schemes within the same employment, even if it involves the expense of bringing the new scheme up to the benefit level of the better of the two old schemes.

The sequence of action required will generally be along the following lines.

1.1 The first decision: insured or self-administered?

(1) Should you use an insured pension contract provided by a life office with or without the provision of administration facilities for routine everyday documentation?

(2) Should you have a self-administered scheme and be free to choose whichever form of scheme management and investment suits your particular needs best?

1.2 The second decision: contract out or stay in the State earnings-related scheme?

This decision, which is discussed further in Chapter 15, involves the following choice:

(1) Whether to contract out of the State earnings-related scheme for earnings between the lower earnings limit (equivalent to the single man's State pension as adjusted from year to year) and the upper earnings limit (approximately 7 × the lower limit figure), or

(2) to contract in to the State scheme for that particular range of benefits.

In April 1984 the lower earnings limit was £34.00 per week and the upper limit was £250.00 per week.

If you are going to contract out, there are three main factors to be resolved, and by law you are required to consult your employees and also keep their trade union representatives (if any) properly informed. The three main factors are as follows:

(1) *Level of benefits.* Would your occupational scheme provide a better range of benefits? This can be achieved either by contracting out *or* by contracting in and topping up with a supplementary occupational scheme. Some actuarial advisers are now taking the view that over-provision of pension benefit (from scheme and State) needs careful re-examination.

(2) *Level of disregard for State basic pension.* The important question of integration with the State scheme benefit structure is considered below (see under 'The fourth decision' (1.4 below)).

(3) *Overall cost.* In the final analysis, it will be the cost (and the flexibility of meeting the cost) of providing the agreed level of benefits which will be the deciding factor.

1.3 The third decision: contributory or non-contributory?

Should the scheme be contributory, i.e. require a contribution from the employee as well as from the employer, or should it be non-contributory and be financed entirely by the employer's contributions?

This is not such a clear-cut decision as may be imagined. The usages of the trade, the levels of pay, the normal span of employment, may all influence the decision as to whether or not the employer should bear the entire cost directly by paying all the contributions to enable the scheme to be properly funded for the benefits promised.

Most private sector schemes have chosen a joint contribution base on the grounds that it gives the employee a better appreciation of the cost of providing him with an income to cover his needs for the remainder of his life after he has retired. The effects of inflation and the consequent erosion of pension values are other important factors which make employees willing to give up a substantial part of their remuneration and to receive it back at a future date in the form of a pension.

1.4 The fourth decision: structure of the scheme

Following on from the first three decisions, which are largely matters of principle, the final decision can now be considered: the scale of benefits and the question of whether or not to integrate with the State scheme. These are two closely interrelated matters.

The heavy cost of providing a final-salary pension scheme led many employers to reconsider the whole structure of their company pension schemes at the time when contracting out of the 1978 State scheme became possible.

By using a deduction equivalent to the current single person's basic State pension when calculating either the initial pensionable salary (for contribution purposes) or the final scheme pension (for pension purposes), an employer could secure a substantial reduction in his contribution outgoings. The argument behind this was that, since the State was already providing the basic State pension for which the National Insurance weekly contribution was paid, it made little sense to provide what was, in effect, two pensions for the same slice of the employee's gross remuneration.

1.4.1 *The fundamental structure of the scheme*

The help of your pension consultant is indispensable at this stage in order to settle the fundamental structure of the proposed pension plan, in so far as it affects the following:

(1) *Benefits.* The rate of pension accrual, e.g. 1/60th or 1/80th for each year of pensionable service, and the differential treatment (if any) of past and future service.

(2) *The funding assumptions.* These cover the actuarial formulae, for future salary and staff movements, to determine the benefits agreed and the contributions necessary to provide those benefits in the light of the special circumstances of each particular fund and its members.

(3) *The contribution structure.* For normal contributions, this would follow after the first two matters set out above have been settled. Separate arrangements may have to be made by the employer to cover any special benefits, e.g. for previously underfunded past service by way

of special contributions which would be over and above the normal contributions.

(4) *Basis of eligibility.* Subject always to the statutory requirement in the Social Security Pensions Act 1975 to give both male and female employees equal access to the pension scheme, careful thought is needed before deciding at what age or at what salary level employees should be allowed or required to enter the company pension scheme. It is also possible, although fortunately only in rare cases, for an employee to have a once-and-for-all choice of two pension schemes, generally with different scales of pension accrual.

1.4.2 *Basis of determining pensionable and final pensionable pay*

Logically, the correct sequence will have been first to decide whether or not there is to be integration with the State scheme. Thereafter, if a deduction (or disregard) has been settled, the further question is to determine if gross PAYE earnings (or net earnings after the disregard) are to be used for setting pensionable salary on which contributions would be charged.

It is still not uncommon, even among the largest companies in the private sector, to find basic earnings, not always with the addition of average overtime earnings, being used to determine pensionable pay, thus excluding a substantial part of normal earnings. *Best practice* is to use gross PAYE earnings with a disregard for the current single man's basic rate of State pension.

Final pensionable pay, on which pension at the time of retirement is based, does not always mean the actual pensionable pay in the final year of service. Most common is a formula using either the average of the last three years in service or the average of the three best consecutive years in the last ten. In practice, there is considerable difficulty in producing a formula satisfactory to all cases; a suggested *best practice* is to have two alternatives, either

(1) the actual rate of pensionable pay in the final year of service, or
(2) the average pensionable pay of the best three pensionable years in the last ten,

whichever is the better.

1.5 The roles played by professional advisers

Best advice would be to appoint all three of your professional advisers, pension consultant, consulting actuary and legal adviser, at the earliest stage. The use you make of these consultants in the early stages will depend largely on the size of the scheme.

Best practice is to concentrate responsibility on your pension consultant without giving him exclusivity; the range of legal and actuarial assistance he can find from his own resources will probably be sufficent for most purposes at this stage. Later, when the scheme is in operation, different and separate advisers will generally be necessary.

A summary of the functions usually handled by the professional adviser, if appointed separately, could be as follows:

(1) *Pension consultant.* The type of scheme and the range of benefits to be given. The range of investments and the use of in-house or external fund managers.

(2) *Consulting actuary.* The funding assumptions most appropriate to your mix of staff and salary levels and to staff movements and salary progression. The funding levels and the contribution rates required to maintain the fund in actuarial balance.

(3) *Legal adviser.* To conduct negotiations with the Superannuation Funds Office (SFO) (the branch of the Inland Revenue responsible for the approval of pension schemes so that tax advantages may be enjoyed) and the Occupational Pensions Board (OPB) (the supervisory body responsible for the preservation and contracting-out requirements) and draft the trust deed, interim and final. To secure Revenue approval for tax-exempt status for contributions and tax reclaim on fund investment income.

Approval of the OPB is only necessary if you wish to contract out of the State scheme or if you subsequently need to amend your rules and modify the benefits.

The most important matters to be covered by your legal adviser in the interim trust deed are:

(a) Compliance with the preservation of benefits requirements under the Social Security Act 1973.

(b) Compliance with the equal access requirements under the Social Security Pensions Act 1975.

(c) The provision of requisite benefits under the Social Security Pensions Act 1975; and

(d) The undertaking to adhere to Revenue limits for benefits.

Prior consultation with the unions and prospective scheme members is mandatory before OPB approval is given.

1.5.1 *Responsibility of parent company*

Your professional consultants and advisers will have spent considerable time in drawing up their recommendations for the type of pension plan they hope you will adopt. In the final outcome, however, it is the company management who will have to bear the responsibility for making the ultimate decisions and accept the substantial costs involved in the operation of an occupational pension scheme.

1.6 Putting the pension scheme into operation

1.6.1 *Consultation with staff and unions*

While obtaining the necessary advice as to the action to be taken *prior* to the start of a pension scheme, consultations with your advisers and the members will undoubtedly have been taking place about contracting out, if applicable, and the manner in which the scheme will be administered after it has received Revenue approval and scheme commencement day is reached.

(1) *Industrial relations/personnel aspects.* Although no employer can be forced to provide an occupational pension scheme, if he decides to have one and contract out, consultation is required by law.

(2) *Agreement with prospective members.* This will involve the pension manager in the planning of the following matters:

    (a) Preparation of announcement literature.

    (b) Briefing by technical experts.

    (c) Establishment of trustee board structure.

    (d) Possible additional pension advisory committee.

    (e) Consultation legally required if contracted out.

The detailed work is dealt with separately below.

1.6.2 *Administrative structure* (see also Chapter 4)

Most insurance companies will provide administration services and pension consultancy for a fee. A considerable amount of preliminary planning is necessary, particularly if large numbers are involved.

Full communication with the impending new membership is essential. All application forms for entry into the new scheme must be completed before contributions are deducted through the payroll. An urgent decision will be required as to the introduction of a computerised benefit record system, either as an in-house facility or provided by an external bureau.

1.6.3 *Trustee structure* (see also Chapter 7)

Most of the decisions about the composition of the trustee board will have been made when the drafting of the trust deed documentation was settled.

The operation of the trustee board activities falls between the secretarial and the administration functions. While the pension scheme manager may often be the secretary of the trustee board, only in a very large scheme should he be given the additional role of a management-nominated trustee.

1.6.4 *Accounting structure* (see also Chapter 13)

Except in the larger schemes, the appointment of a professionally qualified accountant to the pension scheme is not essential. In smaller schemes, the pension scheme manager will often undertake the additional responsibility of keeping the books of account and even preparing the final accounts. It is primarily a book-keeping task until, as the scheme becomes larger, investment records and the dealings of external fund managers have to be incorporated.

Best practice is to appoint a competent accountant when the volume of work so demands, and endeavour to provide some non-accounting work, such as the supervision of property investment, rent collections and service charges in order to give job satisfaction.

The accountant may also be responsible for certain of the computerised functions but only those relating to accounting and investment records. The programming of membership benefits is an involved and time-consuming operation calling for a different range of skills and should be left to the administration manager.

1.6.5 *Investment structure*

In Chapter 10 the problems of investment management are considered, and in Chapter 11 the consequent task of monitoring investment performance is studied in detail.

1.6.6 *Pension scheme management*

The relationship between the management of the fund investments and the control of that management by the pension scheme manager and his board of trustees calls for an administrative structure separate from the ordinary membership administration. This holds good whether fund investment is carried out by the insurers (except in a group contract arrangement), by external fund managers, by in-house fund managers or by an insurance-managed fund unit investment.

Best practice is to have the responsibilities of the pension scheme manager set down when the trustees appoint the external or in-house fund managers and lay down their guidelines. Ultimately, the responsibility for any investment decisions must rest with the trustee board. This is only right since they have an equally onerous and corresponding liability to pay out the benefits from these investments as promised in the rules.

The pension department staff organisation structure must be determined and installed well before D-day. A typical organisation chart for a mature scheme could follow the lines set out in Fig. 1.

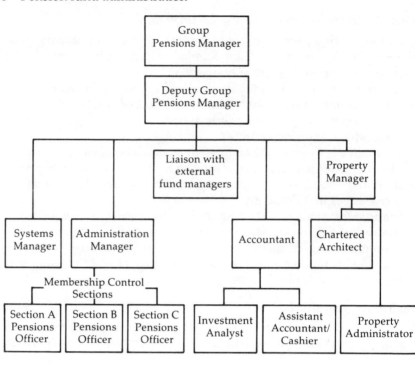

Fig. 1 Specimen organisation chart of a group pensions department. (External investment fund managers have been appointed.)

1.6.7 *Investment performance measurement*

Finally, the time will come for an investment performance analysis system to be set up. This is an essential mechanism, used in conjunction with actuarial valuations of the fund, to determine whether the investments are producing the right quality of asset needed to back up future liabilities of the fund in the form of benefit payments.

1.7 Conclusion

The whole range of professional advisers may not have to be appointed in the first instance – but the ultimate position should always be contemplated. The appointment of a pension scheme manager by the principal employer company is an equally important decision and should be given the proper priority. The 'pursuit of excellence' is the only criterion to be considered in this confined field.

2 Choosing professional advisers

The choice of professional advisers to a pension scheme can best be determined by an examination of the duties they are expected to perform.

The full list of professional advisers could be as follows:

(1) pension consultant
(2) legal adviser
(3) actuary
(4) auditor
(5) investment fund manager
(6) external retained surveyor

This chapter will deal with the range of professional advisers required by a medium-sized self-administered scheme.

In the early stages of a small scheme, particularly of an insured scheme, the services of many of these advisers will be provided under the general administration charge by the insurers. Similarly, the larger firms of consultants will certainly be prepared to offer legal, actuarial and investment advice. It all depends on the size of the scheme as to when it will be more economical to appoint your own individual advisers.

A great deal will also depend on the earlier decisions of principle (covered in Chapter 1) as to whether the scheme should be contracted out, self-administered or insured, contributory or non-contributory. For each of these decisions, the help of your pension consultant and consultant actuary is essential.

Other advisers – legal adviser, auditor and investment fund manager – can then be brought in as required. It cannot be repeated too often: do not hesitate to consult other pension scheme managers whom you know if you wish for a second opinion.

2.1 Advisers' duties

The range of duties required will largely determine how your advisers should be selected and whence they should come. The following matters should be considered:

(1) Have you any existing *in-house legal/tax advisers* already acquainted with the problems of occupational pension schemes? If they are not so acquainted, it is preferable to go outside to experts in those fields. If the outside experts are unsatisfactory, their services can always be terminated.

(2) If you have decided to have a *self-administered* scheme, your administration problem is to that extent settled and dependent on the calibre of the pension staff employed. It may be more economical to use your pension consultant's staff for administration in much the same way as you could use an insurance office if you had chosen to use an insured contract.

(3) The decision as to whether *in-house or external investment managers* should be appointed is generally a matter of size and unlikely to be a problem unless the company already has an investment department.

The appointment of investment managers is found to be an evolutionary process. For a small scheme just starting, it may well be convenient to use an insured contract and have the life office also carry out the administration (see Chapter 5 for the choice of insured contracts).

Later, when the fund builds up and the cost of the insurance overhead for administration work becomes significant, the decision would probably be made to go self-administered. Provision for such a move, without undue penalty, needs to be incorporated in the insured contract.

In the initial stage of self-administered schemes it is probable that external investment fund managers will be appointed (this is covered in detail in Chapter 10), but this should be restricted to the management of negotiable securities and (unless suitable in-house property management facilities are available) separate managers or consultants should be appointed for property investments.

(4) *Property management* covers a wide spectrum of responsibilities; from the search-and-find aspects to the actual investments, through to their management and periodic valuations and ultimately their sale. If suitable in-house facilities are available for any of these property functions, the role of the external property retained surveyor may well be restricted to that of a consultant. The functions of a property consultant are discussed in para. 2.7 below.

2.2 The pension consultant

The appointment of your pension consultant is the first important step in assembling your professional advisers. You will depend on his impartial advice for help in many technical matters relating to the various aspects of your pension scheme, its benefits, its investments and its administration.

Up to comparatively recent times it was customary for pension consultants to be remunerated from their share of the commission or any brokerage they earned from insurance contracts placed by them on behalf of the pension scheme. While this may still be the case for group life and permanent ill health cover, the changeover to self-administered schemes (the National Association of Pension Funds (NAPF) Survey 1983 shows that 69% of all their members' schemes are now self-administered) has resulted in the negotiation of time and cost contracts in the majority of cases. This has had the dual effect of producing a better advice service and of helping to remove suspicion of unethical conduct and a conflict of interest by the consultant.

The appointment of a pension consultant should preferably be on an exclusive basis, but without restriction as to the use of other consultants whenever necessary.

How do you choose your pension consultant? Go to two or three of your commercial friends who already use pension consultants and ask them for their advice. In the final analysis you have to use your own commercial judgement.

2.3 The consulting actuary

The appointment of a consulting actuary is crucial as the consulting actuary is perhaps the most important of all the professional advisers to a pension scheme. On his advice will rest the cost to both the company and the employees and the range of benefits to be provided for scheme members and their dependants.

The actuary may also be responsible for determining the initial mix of the investment portfolio in order to achieve the necessary return of income and capital on the fund. This will enable the contribution requirement to be kept down to a consistent level and so avoid undue fluctuations.

The ultimate responsibility for investment performance must, however, rest with the trustees; they can, of course, make use of expert advice and the choice of investment fund managers is dealt with later in this chapter (see 2.6).

The level of achievement by your investment fund manager will generally be monitored by an external and independent source showing the performance measurement of the whole portfolio on a total return (capital and income) basis. Comparison with other like funds will also be available from any reputable firm giving a performance measurement service. Most of the leading firms of consulting actuaries and pension consultants offer this advice on a fixed fee basis. Some brokers will also provide a performance measurement service free for their own clients, drawing their remuneration from brokerage fees.

2.4 The legal adviser

The appointment of a legal adviser is an essential part of the initial work of starting a new pension scheme. The legal requirements set out in the Finance Act 1970, the Social Security Act 1973 and the Social Security Pensions Act 1975, plus their amendments and the host of statutory regulations and instruments issued under those Acts, are more than sufficient to warrant the appointment of a lawyer with practical experience in pension trust matters.

As has been said already, the requisite legal advice may be available from the specialists already on the staff of the consulting actuaries or the pension consultants. Occasionally, the in-house solicitor may have the necessary specialised experience, but if you go outside it should be to the pension specialist partner or partnership in order to make full use of the best available expertise.

The fees for the initial work in drafting the trust deed and preparing documentation for the SFO and the OPB may be thought substantial, but it is money well spent. If the documentation is done well, subsequent legal charges can be minimised and the relationship changed to a consulting basis.

2.5 Auditors

For a self-administered scheme, *best practice* may be to use the auditors that your parent company uses. In turn, that leads to the question of choosing the starting date of your scheme year, which may also determine the annual date of changing the basic pensionable salaries on which contributions are based. It is of considerable administrative help to choose the right dates; if possible, the change in pensionable salaries should reflect the most up-to-date position, immediately following any annual salary review or the hourly paid wage negotiation date.

The auditors for a large pension scheme may find it convenient to split the annual audit work and have an interim audit during the scheme year, reserving the final audit for systems testing and the final accounts.

The Exposure Draft ED34 issued by the Consultative Committee of Accountancy Bodies goes a long way towards the regularisation of pension scheme accounts and should be studied even in advance of the Statement of Standard Accounting Practice which should be issued during 1984.

The amount of accounting work required from your auditors will largely be determined by the size of your fund and whether it is an insured scheme or not. In general terms, the quality of accounting experience required for keeping the books of a pension scheme is not sufficient to call for a fully qualified accountant, except where it is a self-administered scheme and investment records are involved. *Best practice* for any scheme with over 1,000 members and a fund of over £20 million would be to have a fully qualified accountant and thus confine the auditors' work to the actual audit.

2.6 Investment fund managers

It is a matter primarily related to the size of the fund investment portfolio as to whether external fund managers are appointed or whether investments will be managed by in-house staff. This chapter will deal only with external fund managers, when they should be appointed, and at what stage the question of moving over to in-house management should be considered. (The technical terms of the appointment of external investment fund managers are discussed in Chapter 10.)

An insured contract scheme, or one whose investments consist of insurance-managed fund units, will not normally fall into the type of external fund management now being considered. But consideration should be given to the inclusion of such funds in a performance measurement service so that their performance can be properly monitored and investment changes made where that is possible.

Best practice for self-administered schemes would be to give serious consideration to the appointment of an external fund manager when the portfolio of quoted investments reaches the £20 million mark. Advice as to which fund managers should be approached will be available from your actuaries and also from your pension consultant.

A brief should be prepared and issued to a strictly limited number of managers who will then prepare their presentation to the trustees.

A sufficiently wide range of prospective fund managers should be covered, with presentations from merchant banks and also from stockbrokers and specialist fund managers, including insurance managed funds which have been expanding into this field. A £20 million fund should not be split between more than two managers in the first instance, or three at the outside.

The prospective fund manager should be reasonably forthcoming about the way in which he proposes to handle brokerage charges. The prevailing practice of the acceptance houses, covering all their dealings for pension fund clients with an in-house contract note, is clearly not very satisfactory. A suitable checklist for use by the trustees when considering a fund manager's appointment is given in Chapter 10, para. 10.6.1.

Having made the choice after seeing not more than two prospective fund management presentations in the same day, the letter of appointment should be drawn up in clear language, not necessarily in full legal phraseology, and should be vetted by your legal adviser. The main items it should cover are set out in the draft investment fund management agreement at Appendix 1 and any attempt by the fund manager to impose his own standard form of agreement should be firmly resisted.

2.7 External retained surveyors

The appointment of retained surveyors should be considered as soon as the decision has been reached to make direct property investments. Up to that stage it is probable that property investment will have been made through property unit trusts or insurance-managed fund property units.

Initially it is unlikely that an in-house property manager will have been appointed unless the parent company has a surveyors' department with the necessary expertise. In either case the appointment of an external retained surveyor should be given serious consideration on the grounds that an independent source of advice is essential for providing the balance of judgement when important investment decisions are to be made by the trustees.

Due to the wide divergence of the sources from which property proposals are drawn, the appointment of the existing retained surveyors as external property fund managers is not always to be recommended. If the decision to appoint a property fund manager is agreed then his appointment should follow the procedure set out in 2.6 above with a suitably amended letter of appointment having regard to the professional practices of surveyors.

3 The trust deed

For simplicity, this chapter has been confined to an examination of a definitive trust deed designed to meet the New Code Requirements for Pension Schemes approved under FA 1970, Part II, Chapter II. Mention is also made of the facility of the interim trust deed procedure.

Although a formal document would not appear a mandatory requirement, it would be most unusual under the present SFO practice to find a pension scheme which is not established under irrevocable trusts set out in a formal trust deed together with a schedule of rules defining the benefits and setting out the constitutional framework of the pension trust.

A trust deed need not necessarily be a complex document and it should be set out in such a manner that any reasonably intelligent person can both read and understand it. Reference to some of the trust deeds drafted by modern specialist pension lawyers will support this view. Similarly, the rules can be set out in a logical sequence and made graphically acceptable.

In the principal deed the powers and responsibilities of the trustees are set out. The rules, on the other hand, deal with the benefit entitlements and the obligations of the members. The obligations of the member to the pension scheme and the responsibilities of the trustees to that member rest upon the legally binding agreement set out in the form of application for membership of the scheme.

3.1 Preliminary steps

The preliminary steps which have to be taken before the trust deed and the rules of the scheme are promulgated are as follows:

(1) To decide upon the benefit structure and the classes of employee to be covered.
(2) To decide upon the cost and the division of the contributions between company and employee.
(3) To decide upon the trustee structure and whether the members should appoint/select any trustees.
(4) To decide upon contracting out of the State scheme.

The pensions manager or the scheme administrator designate should be a party to all these discussions, but the decisions should be confirmed formally by an appropriate record in the minutes of the company board.

3.2 The interim trust deed

The complex nature of many pension plans, the number of persons who have to be involved in the establishment of a pension scheme and the timescale required have led to the necessity of having an interim trust deed executed in advance of the definitive document.

The interim trust deed will enable SFO approval to be obtained, but the tax reclaim on fund investment income will still not be allowed unless the trustees enter into a separate bond with the Inland Revenue. The interim deed will give the scheme legal status and, once it is approved by the SFO, contributions by the employer and the members will all be fully allowable for tax relief.

Normally the SFO will accept the members' shortened form of rule book and the preliminary announcement literature as a temporary alternative to the full rules of the scheme which will eventually form an integral part of the definitive trust deed.

For the purpose of obtaining SFO approval, the interim trust deed will have to identify the following:
(1) The parties to the formation of the scheme, i.e. the principal employer company and the trustees as well as provision for the addition of further participating companies and new trustees, also any earlier schemes or trust deeds which are being superseded by the new arrangements.
(2) The undertaking of both parties that the definitive document will conform to all the relevant statutes, e.g. FA 1970 (benefit limits), SSA 1973 (preservation) and SSPA 1975 (equal access).
(3) The power of the parties to amend and substitute the final definitive deed.
(4) The undertaking to procure the execution of the definitive deed within a certain period, usually two years.
(5) The rules regarding benefits and contributions, probably in the form of an announcement to the members.
(6) A wide investment clause.

3.3 The definitive trust deed

This should cover the following:

(1) The parties, i.e. the trustees and the company.
(2) The earlier interim deed and any amendments thereto, also any other deeds containing rights and benefits which have been transferred to the new parties and to the new scheme.
(3) All statutory approvals such as preservation, contracting out (where appropriate), and as an exempt approved fund under FA 1970.
(4) The powers given to the trustees in the interim deed to modify, alter and substitute.
(5) Then, following on the recitals covering the above items, the main clauses of the trust deed relating to the rights and obligations of the trustees, and of the principal and any adhering companies, a detailed list of which is given in Appendix 2.

The modern style of drafting used by experienced pension lawyers represents a considerable improvement on the earlier forms of trust deed. With recognisable main sections and a straightforward contents list in ordinary book style, the layman should be able to find his way easily and identify the clauses for which he is searching. Specimen layouts of a trust deed and rules are shown in Appendixes 2 and 3.

The trust deed and the rules should be kept separate, each with its own contents list, but preferably bound up together in book form, as they both have the same authority. A useful practice is to print the page numbers of the rules in brackets so as to distinguish them from the definitive trust deed.

Each page of both the trust deed and the rules should be headed with clause continuation references at the opening edge and each clause should carry the full reference as shown in the contents list. It is possible to use this form of layout without losing any of its legal efficacy or preventing it from being acceptable to the SFO and the OPB. It should be capable of being used as a book of reference, by both the trustees and any member of the scheme.

If cost considerations permit, the official working copies of the trust deed and rules should be printed single side only to facilitate easy reading, and have space left on the reverse sheets for amendments.

4 The administration of a pension scheme

The administration of a pension scheme involves the use of valuable human and financial resources, which need to be managed efficiently. It brings together the application of the scheme rules, the requirements of legislation, and the obligations and duties of trustees for the ultimate benefit of members and beneficiaries.

This chapter, of necessity, refers only briefly to aspects covered in more detail elsewhere in the book.

The administration of a scheme is governed by the following factors:
(1) The size of the scheme in terms of membership and complexity.
(2) The investment method (whether insured, managed or self-administered).

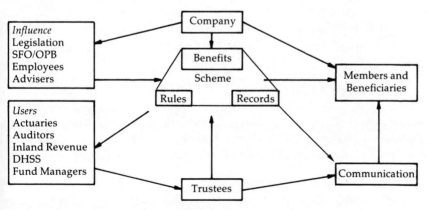

Fig. 2 Plan for the administration of a pension scheme.

(3) The type of benefits provided (in the form of money purchase or average final salary, contributory or non-contributory, contracted out or participating in the State scheme).

Whichever of the above factors apply, the principle remains that the scheme has to be managed and, indeed, the OPB now requires that there should be an officially appointed scheme administrator. So the factor common to all schemes is that services have to be provided either internally (whether centrally or throughout various departments of the company) or externally. They involve the members, the company, the trustees, professional advisers and other external bodies (see Fig. 2).

This chapter does not seek to set out the specific methods to be adopted but deals more with the procedures which should be followed in the administration of a scheme.

There are two principal areas of scheme management:
(1) The secretarial responsibilities relating to trusteeship.
(2) The administration of members' information and benefits.
It is appreciated that there is often no clear distinction between the two areas in many schemes.

Before dealing with each area, some general comments relating to trusteeship are necessary. A more detailed explanation of the responsibilities of trustees is given in Chapter 7.

4.1 Trustees

The trustees (whether corporate or individual) are responsible for the management of the scheme in accordance with the trust deed and rules (together with resolutions made by the trustees) and for carrying out the legal functions relating to the operation of the scheme. The distinction between corporate and individual trustees is meant to denote, in the case of a corporate trustee, the reference to a company or trust corporation and, in relation to individual trustees, people who are collectively responsible for the overall management of the scheme (although some or all of these functions may be delegated to committees). A custodian trustee is sometimes appointed to hold the securities, but such an appointment will not involve any other responsibilities.

4.1.1 Delegation of trustee duties

The trustees of a scheme will probably seek to delegate a number of their duties. This will depend on the size of the operation and the availability of in-house expertise. Any delegated power should be documented by the trustees and the scope of the delegated power clearly specified.

4.1.2 Trustees' discretionary powers

In addition, the scheme will generally provide for the exercise of trustees' discretion, e.g. in relation to death benefits and granting of certain pensions. This again may be delegated to a specific committee or even to local committees whose members would be familiar with the particular circumstances of the individual. Again, the powers delegated and the parameters within which the committees or parties work should be clearly set out.

4.2 Secretarial

This section has grouped the secretarial functions of trusteeship for the purpose of this chapter. Certain aspects included in this section are not specifically a trustee function but are grouped because of their allied nature. In larger funds there may be a clearer division.

The following paragraphs set out the various requirements that should be met and the parties involved to ensure the smooth functioning of the trustee body.

4.2.1 *Meetings*

The trustees should meet regularly and keep minutes of their meetings. The frequency of meetings will be determined by the powers which are delegated and the size of the scheme. An agenda and reports to be discussed need to be prepared for trustees' meetings.

There should be at least one full meeting of the trustee body annually. In addition to the main trustee meeting, there may be committees of management, investment committees and other sub-committees to determine various matters such as the exercise of discretion in cases of death benefits. Minutes must be kept and regular reports submitted by the various committees to the main trustee body which must still bear the ultimate responsibility.

4.2.2 *Trustee appointments*

It is essential to ensure that in the case of individual trustees any vacancy is filled, otherwise the trust may not be able to operate. Filling the vacancy may entail holding an election from representative units or the membership at large. Procedures to be followed should be clearly specified.

4.2.3 *Scheme documentation*

An important function of a scheme is its documentation. Basically, this consists of the trust deed and rules which have to be kept in line with changes in legislation and benefit practice and which form the legal governing document. In addition, the trustees may make resolutions which determine specific practices to be followed within the general powers of the trust deed.

While the trust deed and rules form the legal governing document, most schemes will want to provide members with a simplified explanation of the principal features. It is essential that literature of an explanatory nature is updated on a regular basis, is easy to understand and is readily available to members.

The updating of an accurate set of reference documents from which the basis of the scheme, together with any special provisions, can be quickly ascertained is a necessity in the smooth running of the scheme. This subject is dealt with in detail in Chapter 6.

4.2.4 *Participating companies*

Any change in participating companies requires liaison with the group parent and the particular company. It also involves the execution of legal documents and the collection of information in order to remain within the approval given by the SFO. Consultation by the company with their employees and/or their representatives is always advisable. In the case of a scheme whose members are contracted out, consultation is a statutory requirement and there are also other requirements monitored by the OPB.

4.2.5 *Professional advisers and services*

This has already been dealt with in detail in Chapter 2. Professional advisers to the trustees are remunerated for their services and the terms and conditions under which they operate need to be established and regularly reviewed. The fees can be paid either by the company or by the scheme. This will to some extent depend on how other costs of operation are met. It is not unusual, for example, for administrative expenses to be paid by the company and the costs of investment advisers and transactions to be paid by the scheme.

Some or all of the following advisers will be involved:

(1) *Legal advisers*. These are used in the preparation of the scheme's documents and for advice on legal matters.
(2) *Actuaries*. The actuary's primary duty is to review the financing of the scheme on a regular basis. Information has to be provided to the actuary whether he is in a firm of consulting actuaries or an actuary working within the framework of an insurance company or pension consultants. Frequently, the actuary is also involved in the area of investment and in advising on the implications of benefit changes.
(3) *Accountants*. These operate mainly in relation to the auditing requirements of the scheme. They report to the members and the trustees on the accounts submitted annually. In addition, their services may be required in establishing accounting systems and advising on adequate control of systems.
(4) *Investment advisers*. The use of investment advisers will be determined by whether the scheme is insured or self-administered and depends on the availability of in-house management expertise. In an insured scheme the investment management is provided by the insurance

company. A self-administered scheme or managed fund may establish an investment committee to review policy and appoint specific advisers in the day-to-day management operation of investments.

4.2.6 *Liaison with the employing company*

In Chapter 12, the major areas of contact between the trustees and the employing company are examined in detail. They cover the following:
(1) Procedures for the collection of contributions.
(2) Details relating to members' personal records.
(3) The dissemination of information to members regarding the scheme.
(4) Briefing of company personnel on pension matters. Training facilities should exist either within the employing company or from other organisations. In addition, trustee bodies and consultative committees will sometimes require supplementary training.
(5) In a large fund where there is a separate pensions office, the personnel management of the pensions department may be provided by the company.
(6) The company will require information on the policy and practice to be operated in relation to the scheme, even though this is not a trustee requirement as such.

4.2.7 *Contact with external authorities* (see also Chapter 15)

Of necessity liaison is continuous with the SFO on the operation of the scheme (to comply with regulations and legislation) and the exercise of discretions within Inland Revenue limits. Each change in the trust deed and rules also requires their approval.

Returns have to be submitted to the OPB from contracted-out schemes on an annual basis. Documentation with the inclusion or cessation of participating companies requires OPB approval, and every change in the trust deed and rules also requires their approval.

The local inspector of taxes who deals with the trustee company requires copies of the annual accounts. Tax returns must be submitted. These tax returns are in respect of PAYE tax on pensions paid, tax due on refunds, and lump sums in excess of prescribed limits and reclamation of tax deducted at source on dividends and interest payments.

The Department of Health and Social Security is useful in providing a tracing service where the trustees are unable to locate beneficiaries, e.g. deferred pensioners at retirement. Details of membership termination and statutory requirements also have to be processed for contracted-out schemes.

4.2.8 *Contact with professional associations*

Contact should be maintained with representative bodies such as the NAPF, the Pensions Research Accountants Group and the Pensions

Management Institute in order to keep abreast of developments in the area of pensions, investments, pre-retirement and pensioners' welfare.

The company may also be associated with various trade associations to share pension experiences. Pension managers often form groups with other companies having allied interests for the exchange of information on pension matters.

Information will be required by employee representatives. Similarly, advisory councils or consultative committees within the company, whether specifically existing to deal with pension matters or not, will need to be kept informed.

4.3 Administration

The day-to-day administration of a scheme involves keeping records, preparing or making calculations, paying benefits and providing members and beneficiaries with information. The necessary procedures overlap on common ground, i.e. the rules governing the scheme.

The following paragraphs set out the areas of administration in relation to members and former members, records to be kept and the channels of communication.

4.3.1 *Scheme rules*

The trust deed and rules form the principal governing document and this, together with resolutions passed by the trustees, forms the basis of the scheme's operations. The trustees also need to be kept abreast of 'authoritative changes' by referring to 'Joint Office Memoranda' (as issued by the SFO and OPB), the pensions press and various news-sheets issued by leading consultants/actuaries. The Inland Revenue's Practice Notes (IR12) set out the Revenue's requirements, particularly relating to benefit limits, to which the scheme must conform.

4.3.2 *Members*

Details of the scheme must be given to employees who are eligible for membership. This normally takes the form of an explanatory booklet which will refer to the contributions payable by the member, perhaps specify those payable by the company, and set out the benefits and options on early, normal and late retirement, leaving service and death. If the scheme is contracted out, this must also be indicated and reference included in the member's contract of employment.

Personal details must be recorded and, if possible, the member's date of birth verified. The member's National Insurance number should be noted to enable the scheme administrator to use the Department of Health and Social Security service to verify dates of birth in the event of uncertainty.

The member should also authorise in writing the deduction of contributions from earnings and, if available, complete an 'Expression of Wish' or

'Nomination Form' so that the trustees are advised of the member's wishes as to whom death benefits are to be paid, depending on whether or not payments are discretionary in accordance with the trust deed and rules. A statement of health is sometimes required, particularly when a death benefit is insured.

Any options available to the member should also be explained and recorded. For example, the widow's and orphan's benefits, or the facility to allow members to pay an additional voluntary contribution to enhance the scheme benefits. There may also be a separate sickness benefit scheme. The member should discuss with the company any special requirements concerning his pension benefits.

The question of transferring benefits from a previous employer's scheme should also be discussed. Although it may take a considerable time for the transfer to be made, the members should be advised of the procedure. They need to know that the decision to transfer is solely their own, subject to the approval of both sets of trustees, and that they should compare the alternative benefits available from their previous scheme against the benefits that the transfer value will purchase in the new scheme. This may be a specified pension or added years, enhancing pensionable service in the new scheme.

4.3.3 *Former members/beneficiaries*

Members leave the scheme for one of three reasons: they may leave, retire or die.

4.3.3.1 *Early leavers*. The rules will set out the options available on termination of employment. There are generally three options: a refund of contributions, deferred pension or transfer to another scheme:

(1) *Refunds of contributions.* Qualification for refunds of contributions will be dependent on the rules subject to 'Preservation and Contracting-Out Requirements' and refunds may be reduced by certain permissible (statutory) deductions to comply with preservation requirements. The treatments of transfers-in from other schemes will affect qualifying service for determination of whether a refund is payable. The scheme liability will normally cease after the payment of a refund, but could continue if a part-refund is made with the balance in the form of deferred pension.

(2) *Deferred pensions.* The member must be advised of the normal starting date, the amount of the deferred pension, and its apportionment between Guaranteed Minimum Pension (GMP) and any excess, when the pension becomes payable and at what intervals (e.g. monthly in advance).

Details should also be given of any increase in pensions, the earliest date when the pension is payable and any actuarial reduction which may apply on early retirement together with benefits payable on death before and after pension payment commences. Important legislation relating to the escalation and calculation of deferred pensions is likely to be brought into effect in 1984/85.

The member should be given a statement containing all the above information and recommending that he should contact the trustees prior to his attaining normal retirement age. It is also important to suggest that the member retains the deferred pension statement together with other important papers as the deferred pension may not be paid for many years, and in the event of his death prior to normal retirement date it will be made clear whether a benefit would be payable in respect of the deferred pension, such as a dependant's pension or merely a refund of contributions after the Widow's Guaranteed Minimum Pension (WGMP) has been met.

(3) *Transfers-out*. Most schemes are capable of taking in and paying out transfer values to and from other approved schemes. One of the problems is that a contracted-out scheme may not transfer the GMP element to a scheme which participates in the State scheme, or to those who are unwilling to accept the GMP liability.

It may, however, be possible to retain the GMP/Equivalent Pension Benefit liability as a deferred pension and to transfer the excess.

On leaving a scheme the member must be advised of his deferred pension rights so that he is able to compare the alternative benefits offered to him by the administrator of the new scheme based on the transfer of the actuarial cash value of the deferred pension. If the member wishes to proceed, he must authorise the transfer to take place in writing.

(4) *Miscellaneous*. There may be some members who have not left the company but have withdrawn from membership of the scheme because of transfer to part-time employment, or have declined to take an option to transfer to an improved scheme. If the company scheme is contracted out, such members will generally have to revert to a contracted-in status and pay full State scheme contributions.

4.3.3.2 *Retirement*. The following options apply at retirement age:
(1) *Pension*. Members eligible for retirement benefits are those who attain pensionable age either while still in employment or as deferred pensioners. The benefits applicable to each will be defined within the rules.

In addition, members may retire voluntarily on attaining an earlier age, but such payments are usually subject to a reduction.

A scheme may provide for retirement due to incapacity by reason of varying degrees of ill-health. Expert medical advice is required to establish eligibility for permanent ill-health retirement as some form of enhancement is often applied in such cases. Alternatively, there may be a permanent ill-health insurance under which the sick member still remains a member of the scheme, continuing to build up pension benefits. Incapacity pensions are generally payable for life but in certain situations the rules allow the trustees to review the eligibility for such a pension after a period of time.

(2) *Lump sums.* This option enables the member to give up part of the annual pension in exchange for an immediate tax-free lump sum. A retiring member needs to know the amount which needs to be exchanged for any given amount of lump sum. The member should consider the level of total income in retirement, including possible increases, before deciding whether or not to commute part of his pension.

(3) *Other options.* A further option is often given at retirement which is the opportunity to surrender part of the member's pension for an additional pension to a dependant on death of the member. The consequences should the nominee pre-decease the member must be clearly explained.

(4) *State benefits.* The various State benefits should also be explained either directly to the member or by the issue of the relevant Department of Health and Social Security leaflets which are readily available.

The method of payment of pension is of particular importance to a pensioner. The common methods are as follows:

(1) Cheque – sent direct to the pensioner.
(2) Bank transfer – by Bankers' Automated Clearing Service (BACS) or by credit transfer direct to the pensioner's bank account.
(3) Giro transfer – direct to the pensioner's Girobank account.

Often the trustees will not wish to be directly involved in the payment of a pension and may use a payment service. Certain commercial firms are established which will make payments on the trustees' behalf. Payments of pension in cash should be avoided wherever possible because of the risk of fraud.

Another method of payment involves an insurance company. If pensions are paid direct by the insurer acting as agent for the trustees, the method of payment will often be outside the trustees' control, but will have been approved by them.

It is important for audit purposes that pension payments are strictly controlled. *Best practice* is to pay by cheque or credit transfer to a bank or Post Office Giro account which ensures that the pensioner has to satisfy an independent and intermediate source as to his continued existence.

4.3.3.3 *Death.* On the death of the member or former member, contact with the family of the deceased is important. Often it is possible to arrange for a company welfare officer to visit the family; if not, then written contact should be made. The trustees will require sight of the member's or former member's birth certificate (if not already seen), marriage certificate (if applicable), death certificate (or the coroner's certificate where there is to be a post-mortem examination), together with the birth and marriage certificates of any children.

Other important matters which should then be dealt with are as follows:

(1) *Lump sum death benefits.* These are usually payable under the discretionary powers of the trustees and do not form part of the deceased's estate for capital transfer tax purposes. The member will normally have completed an 'Expression of Wish' form which will be of help to the trustees.

An advance of part of the lump sum can usually be made without the necessity of full documentation if the case is straightforward.

(2) *Dependant's pension.* In many schemes the trustees have the power of discretion to pay the whole or part of the death benefits to a dependant as an alternative or in addition to that payable to the spouse of a deceased member. This overcomes any argument about widower's pensions.

The definition of a 'dependant' will be found in the scheme rules and should be as wide as can reasonably be prescribed (usually, 'anyone not necessarily a relative who was wholly or partly dependent financially on the deceased at the time of his death').

The full facts of the case must be presented to the trustees, with any further relevant information which the local management can obtain, to assist the trustees to decide the way in which they should exercise their discretion.

(3) *Child allowances.* The SFO permits children's allowances to be paid beyond normal school leaving age while the child is in full-time education up to age 25 or is mentally or physically handicapped. It is essential to receive proof that the full-time education is continuing by means of a certificate from the parent/guardian or the school principal.

(4) *Infant settlements.* It is not unusual to find that the trustees may wish to cover the payment of the lump sum benefits to infant beneficiaries by a formal deed of settlement, primarily as a means of protecting both their interests. The form of the deed should preferably be settled by the scheme legal adviser.

Best practice is not to have any company or pension department representatives as trustees to the deed but to use the nearest acceptable relation and either an established firm of solicitors or a bank trustee company to give the necessary continuity.

4.4 Membership records

In order to process benefits for members and other beneficiaries, extensive information relating to each member's history is required. To create and maintain such details there must be an exchange of information between the company and the administrator (if this is carried out externally as a separate function). In addition, information has to be passed to the DHSS in respect of those schemes contracted out.

Methods of record-keeping will vary with the size of the scheme (and the company) from manual records, cards or schedules to sophisticated computer records which may be available for on-line access and updating (see also Chapter 13, para. 13.11). With ever increasing storage problems, microfilming will no doubt feature. A typical form of computerised membership record which has been in use for some years is shown in Appendix 4. Other more sophisticated records are now becoming available with on-line presentation facilities.

The aim should be a comprehensive record-keeping system which traces a person's history throughout his or her scheme membership. Records will consist of the following:
(1) Personal information which will remain relatively constant throughout membership.
(2) Financial details relating to earnings and contributions.
(3) Benefits paid or payable on various dates.
(4) Contracting-out information, if appropriate.
Details of the information requirements under each of the various categories mentioned above are set out below. The level of details will be determined by the needs of a particular scheme.

4.4.1 *Personal*

Initially, information will be obtained when a member joins a scheme (usually by completing an application form) and supplemented by subsequent changes. The following details should be included:

Name and initials	Branch location/work site
Sex	Expression of Wish (Nomination)
Marital status	details
Date of birth	Dependant(s): name and sex
Date joined company	Dependant(s): date of birth
Date joined scheme	Dependant(s): relationship
Date of birth of spouse	Present status, e.g. member/
Normal retirement date	deferred/pensioner/
National Insurance No.	dependant
Membership No.	Date of status change

4.4.2 *Financial*

Details retained should include a year-by-year record of the following:

Earnings and pensionable pay
Member's normal contributions and interest
Member's additional voluntary contributions
Periods of pensionable service – current schemes
                               – previous schemes
                               – transfers-in
Period of 'qualifying service'
Additional benefits from – previous schemes, e.g. deferred pension
                               – current scheme
Any underlying benefits guarantee (this information can often be held
in the form of notes)

4.4.3 *Benefits*

On termination of employment for whatever reason and subsequent retirement or death, details of benefits paid and those continuing in payment are required. Certain payments may require review, e.g. dependant's pension ceasing at age 18 or certain payments made only to State retirement age. The range of details should include the following:

Total contributions and interest
Tax payable
Refundable contributions
Transfer value
Continuing lump sum death benefit
Pension payable (may be split between various types)
Commencement date of pension
Dependant's contingent pension
Maximum cash available at normal retirement date
Cash taken at retirement and pension surrendered
History of pension and increases
Basis of pension increases
Date of expiry of pension instalment guarantee
Frequency of pension payment
Augmented benefit and cost
Action dates (e.g. attainment of age 18)

4.4.4 *Contracting out*

If a scheme is or has been contracted out, further records need to be kept. It is important that the member's name and National Insurance number correspond to that on the DHSS record and that the employee's contracted-out National Insurance contributions are advised by the company to the Inland Revenue on form P35 (or equivalent P14 return). It is recommended that the following records are maintained so that the DHSS calculations can be verified:

Date contracted out
National Insurance contribution history
National Insurance contribution category
Certified amount
Contributions Equivalent Premium
Guaranteed Minimum Pension
Widow's Guaranteed Minimum Pension
Revaluation basis of Guaranteed Minimum Pension
Limited Revaluation Premium
Equivalent Pension Benefit ⎱ for schemes contracted out prior to April
Payment in lieu   ⎰ 1975
Any linked qualifying periods of contracted-out service

The scheme members' records will be used for a variety of purposes, such as the following:
(1) *Actuarial valuations.* This will include data for current members, former members and details of pensioners, together with changes in status during the periods between valuations.
(2) *Costings.* Details of particular sections of the membership may be required to enable amendments to be made, e.g. details of pensioners so that pension increases can be paid.
(3) *Group life assurance.* Distribution of membership by sex, age and salary, particularly for insured schemes.
(4) *Terminations.* To calculate members' and dependants' benefits.

4.4.5 *Accounting*

Within the administrative function, accounting and investment records have to be maintained and the fund managed. This area should not be overlooked in planning the management of a scheme and is dealt with in detail in Chapter 13.

4.4.6 *Communication* (see also Chapter 6)

Administration involves liaising with members and their beneficiaries. Most communication is in written form and includes:
(1) Booklets outlining details of the scheme.
(2) Benefit statements during membership and on termination, details of options, etc.
(3) Information relating to the management of the scheme, e.g. Report and Accounts.

4.5 Conclusion

The administration of any pension scheme covers many disciplines. The key to efficiency is being aware of the requirements and able to meet the demands of members, beneficiaries, the trustees, the company and other interested parties.

5 Insured pension contracts

Historically, an insured pension contract meant that the insurance company took in age-related premiums in exchange for guaranteeing payment of a pension at an employee's retirement age. In a small way, that role still exists. But now, factors such as inflation, the advent of pension schemes based on an employee's final salary, the market demand for measurable investment performance and the competitive pressure of the concept of the directly invested scheme have expanded the role of the insurance company in the pensions field.

For larger schemes, for example, insurance companies have devised the managed fund, offering units in a selection of equities, gilts, property, overseas and specialist investment funds. For very large schemes, they have devised the segregated fund which, by giving a scheme its own investment portfolio, affords it an investment opportunity very similar to the services offered by merchant banks.

Alongside these investment methods, the insurance companies operate the full range of administrative, investment, actuarial, documentation and other services, as well as their traditional service of insuring the risk benefits, such as death-in-service and prolonged disability cover.

At the other extreme, the insurance companies have retained their traditional function of providing pension schemes for individuals and for very small groups of employees, particularly senior employees such as directors. Such schemes can be run with insurance guarantees or can expose their members to the risk – and potentially higher reward – of unit-linked investment for their contributions. A full description of such schemes is given in Chapter 14.

This chapter is mainly concerned with the operation of the mainstream insured pension contract used by many thousands of small, medium and some very large United Kingdom pension funds.

5.1 Insured group pension contracts

Essentially, the insured group pension contract is a contract which gives the following:
(1) Guarantees of both capital and limited level of investment interest.
(2) The expectation of bonuses.
(3) A guaranteed cash-to-pension conversion rate.
Different insurance companies express their contracts in different ways, but the customary elements are as follows:
(1) The contributions invested for pension purposes year by year are fully guaranteed as capital except to the extent that they have to be used to pay for the setting-up of pensions and other benefits.
(2) The first interest addition made annually to the invested contributions is also guaranteed, although not for all time. For example, the size of the addition might be guaranteed for three years, although it might apply to all contributions paid during those years for another 12 years. The addition can be a fixed percentage amount or it can be more directly related to actual investment conditions, e.g. half the mean of certain specified high coupon gilts.
(3) The second interest addition is not guaranteed. This is the bonus element which represents the particular scheme's share in the insurance company's disposable surplus. The bonus will therefore reflect the insurance company's investment earnings on its life and annuity fund. However, another bonus reflects the growth in the underlying value of this fund's investments and may either be given as an annual addition to the income-related bonus or as a special terminal bonus allocated to the scheme when an employee comes to take his pension at retirement.
(4) Although in practice pensions are nearly always bought at retirement age on the insurance company's current immediate annuity rates (or possibly on another company's rates), the contract guarantees (for five years, say) an annuity purchase rate, which would prove useful in an era of low interest rates.

The precise shape of these elements varies from one insurance contract to another as insurance companies devise new contracts or adapt old ones in response to market demand. What they have in common, however, is measurability, since each can be rendered down into a quantifiable track record.

5.2 Comparison of insured and self-invested funds

The most striking difference between an insured contract on the one hand and the direct investment or managed fund method on the other is, of course, the guarantees which the former gives. But there is another, less obvious, difference. Investment return depends primarily on the investing institution's experience of general economic conditions and its own investment success. For a managed or directly invested scheme, the impact of the inevitable ups and downs is immediate and, from time to time, even dramatic. For an insured contract, however, the impact is in practice apt to be smoothed and the sharpest fluctuations in investment results avoided.

5.2.1 *Deposit administration contracts*

The simplest method of applying pension contributions is called 'deposit administration'. All the contributions flow unearmarked into the pension scheme's common pool and it is into that pool that guaranteed interest and bonus additions go each year.

This, apart from the guaranteed interest, is very close to how directly invested schemes operate. Like them, it is important not to have to realise investments to pay for pension purchases. This explains why these purchases are made, in the case of insured deposit administration contracts, from current pension contributions and not from the pool of invested contributions.

5.2.2 *Controlled funding contracts*

The other main method of applying contributions is called 'controlled funding'. Although the investment effect is much the same as deposit administration, the technique is to use the invested contributions to buy pension rights for all the employees, starting with the oldest and working down the age range as far as the contributions will go. Investment yield in this case provides the extra money with which further pension purchase can be made.

5.3 Actuarial aspects of funding

Whatever the technique, it is important to understand that to speak of the *cost* of an insured pension scheme (or of a managed or directly invested scheme, for that matter) is to speak imprecisely. Broadly, the actuary will recommend a rate for the company's contributions which he believes is right on the assumption he makes and the funding objective he favours. Another actuary will almost certainly recommend a different rate, but this is because his assumptions and his target are different, even if only slightly.

For example, the first actuary may assume that the growth in pensionable salaries will be outpaced by the investment return by $\frac{1}{2}$% per annum and reckons to bring the scheme over a certain period to the point when its liabilities are exactly matched by its assets. If the second actuary puts the gap a little wider and proposes a longer period for the matching, his recommended outlay is therefore lower.

It is not, therefore, a matter of the cheapest quotation, because the liabilities will still emerge whatever the outlay. It is entirely a matter of the pace at which these liabilities should be funded for, especially the liability for pensions awarded for employment before the scheme starts. Ideally, the pace should be even, without any violent upward and downward jolts.

5.4 Discontinuance and withdrawal

Appraising what it is like to enter into a contract is important. It is also important to appraise what it is like to get out of it again. Some companies, although not all, feel that a point, often subjectively chosen, may come when they should go it alone with the risk-taking inherent in an insurance-company-managed fund or in direct investment.

The question is: how locked in is the company which wants to make the move, since it would usually want to put the assets built up so far in the same place as its future contributions? As with investment yield, different contracts say different things. One might confine itself to the same outcome as if the scheme was being entirely wound up. In that case, the value placed on the assets would be used to buy deferred annuities on the insurance company's current rates for each member of the scheme, to be paid out as and when he or she retires.

However, there are usually other options. One is to withdraw the money standing to the scheme's credit over, say, ten years, one-tenth in the first year, one-ninth of the balance in the second year and so on until the assets (plus the continuing investment interest, probably at a reduced rate for the bonuses) are entirely paid away.

Another option is to take a single lump payment, perhaps spread over a short period (two years, say) if it is particularly large. How this sum compares with the cash assets built up so far depends in part on the insurance company's appreciation of current economic conditions. It often depends, too, on the precise nature of the move out of the insured contract. For example, the lump sum is likely to be enhanced if the move is to the same insurance company's managed fund.

5.4.1 Charges

The contract's discontinuance provisions are not guaranteed to last for all time. A short-term guarantee, typically lasting five years, may be found. The same kind of guarantee is usually found for the administration charges which the insurance company levies on each year's pension contributions before they are invested. Again, the detail of these charges varies, but a common picture is one of three charges:

(1) An index-linked charge for the scheme as a whole, presently amounting to, say, £1,000.
(2) An index-linked charge for each member, presently amounting to, say, £11 for each current member and £2 for each member who has left service with preserved pension rights.
(3) A percentage of the pension contributions, presently $3\frac{1}{4}\%$, say, part of which is used to remunerate the company's pensions adviser, who would rebate it if he charges fees for his services.

Some contracts use special refinements for calculating service charges. One common refinement is to give some kind of reduction when contributions are running at above a certain annual level. Administrative charges are nearly always expressed in this overt manner, or something close to it, by deposit administration contracts – other types of insured pension contracts tend not to do so. There is, however, one main exception: charges are one of the several elements which are embedded in the age-related premiums for insured death-in-service benefits and prolonged disability income cover.

5.5 The standard servicing package

The type of charges just mentioned for pension administration are for a standard services package. This includes the following:

(1) *Funding.* The insurance company actuary advises on, for example, the rate at which the company should contribute; carries out a valuation and reports every three years (sometimes more frequently as a matter of routine or because some special event makes it necessary); recommends on the size of transfer payments for individual employees, or groups of them, to other pension schemes; and tests the take-up of early retirement pensions against the general financial well-being of the scheme.
(2) *Revenue negotiation.* The insurance company obtains the Inland Revenue's tax approval for the scheme at its outset, submits scheme alterations for continued approval and ensures that tax requirements (and the requirements of the OPB relating to preserved pensions for early leavers and contracting out) are met at all times.
(3) *Documentation.* The insurance company supplies explanatory booklets for the members, formal rules and, for the company's solicitor, drafts of the legal documents.
(4) *Administration.* This, always the largest part of the services package, includes record-keeping, claims calculations, pension payments and employee benefit statements.

5.6 Comparative advantages of insured contracts

An insurance company is not the only qualified supplier of the above services. However, each service put out to another supplier carries a price-tag which, along with the quality and scope the supplier gives, needs to be appraised by the pension scheme manager.

This is also true of the risk benefits: the lump sum, survivor pension and children's benefit paid on death-in-service and the prolonged disability income cover. Some larger schemes carry all or part of these risks themselves. Insuring the risk is the usual method, although not necessarily with the same company which invests the pension contributions. Some schemes prefer to shop around for the best rates. However, the gross premium charged for the risk is not the only thing to consider. Also to be considered are the return-of-premium arrangement when claims are lighter than expected; the insurance company's view of giving cover without medical enquiry; in the case of disability cover, the definition of disability qualifying for benefit and exclusions from successful claims; and the length of time (e.g. three years or five years) for which premium rates are guaranteed.

5.7 Factors determining choice of scheme management

Over the years, the most important pensions question for a company's decision-makers has proved to be: what factors should be taken into account when considering which of the insured, managed or directly invested roads to go down? There are six main factors:

5.7.1 *Convenience*

If a company wants to run a pension scheme without having to give members of its staff the additional burden of running its day-to-day administration, buying in all the expert advice the scheme needs and, most important, taking investment decisions, then an insured pensions contract is an obvious choice. This is because the insurance company looks after the complete running of the scheme, except for the solicitor's role and the essential paper-work which only the company's pensions administrator can do.

5.7.2 *Size*

Plainly, a company setting up a scheme for the first time for its 25 employees could not easily contemplate the risk-taking inherent in the non-insured approach. Equally, it is rare to find a company with over 2,500 pensionable employees relying on insurance guarantees. But it is not sensible to lay down any mechanical rule which states that after a scheme has reached a certain size, measured by its membership, its assets or its current level of contribution income (or all three), it should automatically change from an insured contract to a managed or directly invested basis. The insurance company almost certainly has a measurement criterion below which it would regard change as being untimely. But much more to the decision-making point are the next factors.

5.7.3 *Guarantees*

Managed and directly invested schemes are completely exposed, for good or ill, to the volatility of investment results. These depend in part on the investment manager's skill, but much more on external economic events beyond his control. Such events affect the insurance company, but because of the investment and other guarantees it gives, the insured scheme has a permanently valuable insulation. Naturally, guarantees have to be paid for and the company must take its own view on their value.

5.7.4 *Pooling*

Insured and managed funds depend in large part for their investment success on, first, the judicious spread of their portfolios across the whole range of equities, gilts, property and other more specialised investments (e.g. overseas) and, second, the skilful selection of investment within these sectors. For smaller schemes, which could hardly ever obtain the most rewarding kind of investment mix by themselves, taking a share in the results of a large piece of insurance company action offers a less risky outcome than direct investment.

5.7.5 *Investment muscle*

Large investing institutions like insurance companies have access to special investment offers denied to all but the very largest directly invested schemes. This is particularly true of property, which is a necessary part of any well-balanced scheme portfolio as a useful hedge against inflation.

5.7.6 *Performance*

Bearing in mind that investing for pensions is a long-term activity and should always be seen in that light, the performance of investing institutions is generally seen as what ultimately counts.

An insured contract's performance is as measurable as that of others of the same type as well as that of any kind of investment manager. Indeed, it is usual to find a specific reference to an insured scheme's own performance in the insurance company's report to its policyholders. Naturally, when it comes to making a choice, performance has to be seen as part of the complete range of services which a pension scheme needs for its continued success.

5.8 Additional voluntary contributions

Insured contracts have a special role in the area of additional voluntary contributions (AVCs). It is possible to run an AVC facility within a directly invested scheme, perhaps exposing the contributions directly to investment conditions. However, security for an employee's personally volunteered contributions is widely seen as essential. This accounts for the great popularity among schemes of all kinds for a separate insured AVC contract which gives them guarantees of capital and investment return with the prospect of bonuses in addition.

5.9 Small self-administered schemes for directors

An insured contract is an obvious choice in other areas, too. For example, there has been in recent years a considerable growth in the number of 'small self-administered pension schemes'. These are set up, usually by the directors of director-controlled companies under the provisions of the Income and Corporation Taxes Act 1970, section 266, as a means both of making provision for retirement and death benefits and of permitting a degree of investment back into a company's business through, for example, loans and property acquisitions.

Part of the pension contributions would be invested conventionally, often meaning insurance policies either with capital and investment guarantees or based on the unit-linked approach. Frequently, the insurance company is appointed 'pensioneer trustee', the expert person whom the Inland Revenue insists is appointed to join the ordinary trustees as a condition of the scheme's approval.

This specialised area of pension benefit provision is examined in detail in Chapter 14.

5.10 Administration arrangements

5.10.1 *Insurance company cover*

Some insurance companies will also provide administration cover for company pension schemes and so relieve the trustees of the responsibility for all the routine procedures although not the investment decisions. Although a charge will be made for this service, it may still be more economical for a company which does not run to a fully-fledged pensions department.

5.10.2 *Buying out the GMP liability*

Another example of the way in which insured contracts have been diversified came to the fore soon after the contracting-out option took effect in 1978. As employees left service, large numbers of guaranteed minimum pensions began to accumulate in the records of contracted-out schemes or, when service had been short, were brought back into the State scheme at what often seemed a disproportionately high cost. An insured contract can be used, with savings in both administrative time and cost, to take over this complex liability and, if the rules so permit, the whole liability for early leavers' preserved pension rights.

5.10.3 *Section 32 personal insured contracts for deferred pensions introduced by Finance Act 1981*

A further example of the diversification of insured contracts is the 'Section 32 annuity' which has provoked a great deal of interest during the debate about protection for the pension rights of someone who changes his job. Under Section 32, the individual scheme member is able to arrange for the transfer value of the preserved pension, which would otherwise have been left behind in his ex-employer's scheme, to be paid into an individual pension policy issued by an insurance company. The lump sum paid out at retirement date is governed by Inland Revenue regulations relating to the protection of the GMP, but as it is derived from a with-profits policy, there is a good, although not guaranteed, chance that it will be able to secure an annuity larger than the preserved pension he would otherwise have collected from his former scheme.

5.11 Conclusion

This chapter has been mainly concerned with the pension scheme which promises pensions based on its members' final salaries. Some companies, particularly smaller companies, prefer to promise pensions which are directly based on the proceeds at retirement of jointly invested contributions. A typical 'money purchase' scheme would have the employee contribute 3%, say, of his earnings and his company another 5%, say. At retirement, he would be able to buy tax-approved retirement benefits with the cash standing in his own individual account. Clearly, it would not be wise to leave such an employee's pension future entirely exposed to investment risk. Money purchase schemes are therefore obvious candidates for an insurance company's guarantees of capital and interest.

6 Disclosure to members

The term 'disclosure' in the context of pension schemes has been taken to mean the communication of all necessary and relevant information about the company pension scheme to the company's employees and to the scheme members.

In this chapter we will examine the provision of such information by the following:
(1) The company management.
(2) The trustees of the pension scheme.
(3) The pension scheme manager or administrator on behalf of both the company and the trustees.

The types of information to be considered will be as follows:
(1) General information about the scheme and any changes in the scheme rules.
(2) General information about the pension fund and its investments.
(3) Particular information about the benefits of the individual member, both in service and after service.
(4) Special information for the use of the pension department staff in communicating the above information.

Communication should develop from a whole-hearted conviction held by both the company management and the trustees of the pension scheme that it is in the best interests of the scheme members for full and proper and timely disclosure to be made about the pension scheme which is the concern of both the company and the members.

Communication, as will be seen later in this chapter, is a two-way process of disclosure, involving the specialised training of all engaged in the communication process – company management, trustees and members.

6.1 Facilitating the process of communication

The following are useful in facilitating the process of communication:

6.1.1 *The written word*

The basic scheme documentation should be reproduced in an edited but accurate form which should be attractive and intelligible to the ordinary member.

The same comments apply to the Annual Report and Accounts (whose format is dealt with in detail in Chapter 13) and to any pictorial newssheet summary, which can on occasion be incorporated usefully as a foreword to the main Report and Accounts.

6.1.2 *Speech*

Formal and informal meetings are an inevitable part of the administration process of any pension scheme. The golden rule is that they should be held at a suitable time of day (e.g. not after a substantial lunch) and in a place where all those present can feel free to take an active part in the discussions.

These meetings should be fully publicised so that there can be no feeling of unwillingness on the part of the management staff responsible for setting up the meeting or on the part of the members attending, if it is the wish that the meeting should serve a useful and constructive purpose.

6.1.3 *Audio-visual and other electronic aids*

The development of the audio-visual slide/film presentation has revolutionised the field of pensions communication and has led directly to the great improvement of both written and spoken aids.

6.1.4 *The professional attitude of well-trained pension department staff*

It may no longer seem necessary to stress this particular aspect in view of the remarkable progress that has been made in securing the large numbers of professionally (PMI) trained and qualified pension staff now required by the ever-growing number of occupational pension schemes.

The days when pensions staff had to learn by hard-earned and poorly rewarded practical experience have largely disappeared. However, without the work of the staff who trained in this way, many of the largest schemes in the United Kingdom would still be hard put to it to function efficiently, despite all the progress made in the provision of computerised pension and payroll programs. The pressures of the last decade in the pensions field have literally meant that only the most competent could survive.

6.2 Types of information required and stages of disclosure

6.2.1 *On entry into employment*

It is now a statutory requirement (Contracts of Employment Act 1981) that full details of any pension scheme, including eligibility and liability for membership, should be given to all new employees who will become eligible for membership, at the same time as the terms of the contract of employment are made available.

All that is necessary at the stage of entry into employment is a suitably phrased two-page leaflet set out in layman's language, giving a general outline of the scheme benefits and the cost of contributions, if any, and the time before eligibility is completed and membership is available. The information leaflet should also state whether the scheme is contracted out of the State scheme.

After the employment has actually started, the personnel department should be responsible for bringing to the notice of all employees details of the methods of their representation on the trustee board and on any pension advisory committees.

In some companies where the contract of employment does not specify that membership of the company pension scheme, when eligible, is obligatory, personnel departments sometimes take the precaution of having an application form for subsequent entry into the pension scheme signed at the time of making the above information available. However, unless this is accompanied by evidence of birth and marital status, it does not serve any useful purpose, especially bearing in mind the normal heavy turnover of staff during the first year of any employment, and the movements between departments.

6.2.2 *On entry into the pension scheme*

To avoid problems of identifying benefits due at a date long distant in the future, this stage of documentation must be carried out carefully and completed wherever possible in advance of the actual date of entry into pensionable service, i.e. the date from which all future pension benefits will be calculated.

Some organisations, particularly in the public sector, provide for immediate entry into the pension scheme upon taking up the employment. There are certain administrative advantages, such as avoiding the necessity for the steps outlined above, but the cost disadvantage to the company in dealing with the heavy turnover of staff during their first year of employment is thought to more than outweigh any administrative convenience.

An alternative and preferable solution is to give free life cover, i.e. without contribution from the employee, until he actually becomes a member of the pension scheme and is eligible for the normal scheme death benefit cover.

The essential procedures for entry into membership of a pension scheme have been referred to in Chapter 4. In Chapter 13 reference is made to the facilities now available from computer programs for both payroll and pension scheme records.

Time is of the essence in completing the preliminary documentation for what is clearly a financial contract of the utmost importance to the employee. With his application form for membership, the employee should have a suitable booklet outlining all the main facets of scheme membership and giving examples of how those benefits would work out in practice.

The old style of rule book is no longer in vogue. In its attempt to cover the benefits in overfull legal language, it often created more misunderstanding, or worse still actually discouraged examination by the ordinary employee. The modern scheme booklet, often in colour and including graphic illustrations, should be both interesting and capable of being understood without the assistance of a pensions expert. It will, of course, always refer to the overriding authority of the actual rules attached to the governing trust deed as amended from time to time.

The application form, on the other hand, is a legal document and must be precisely phrased, so as to avoid any misleading terms. It represents the offer by the prospective member to the trustees to make contributions (where applicable) in return for the benefits which will be available on the grant of membership. The counterpart of this contract, and the completion of the exchange, is the formal acceptance of the application by the trustees, generally expressed by a Certificate of Membership signed by the trustees or the scheme manager or administrator. This should also give details of any past service credits brought into the scheme.

Each stage of this contractual process must be made manifestly clear to the employee.

6.2.3 *While in service*

Despite the importance of giving full information about the pension scheme to the employee before he actually joins the scheme, there should be no relaxation in the process of disclosure once he has become a member. It is in connection with this much longer stage that much justified criticism has been made in the past about the inaction of pension scheme management and trustees. Their duty and, indeed, obligation is to dispel this criticism by making full and proper disclosure about the following:

(1) The general benefits as expressed in the trust deed and rules as amended from time to time.
(2) The investment of the contributions and the financial state of the fund.
(3) The ways and means whereby members can express their dissatisfaction concerning the affairs of the scheme.
(4) The specific benefits promised to the individual members and what they actually mean.

The documentation required to cover these matters is of vital importance and any attempt to gloss over items which are unpleasant or unsatisfactory will only cause strain on employee relations.

The principal documentation to fulfil a proper standard of disclosure is as follows:

6.2.3.1 *The trust deed and rules.* It is very uncommon to find every member being issued with a copy of the full trust deed and rules. Indeed, it might well be counter-productive and the wealth of legal phraseology would tend to confuse rather than throw light on technical matters to the ordinary lay enquirer.

In Chapter 3, emphasis has been laid on the importance of a proper contents list for a modern-style trust deed. Provided there is easy access to copies of the basic deed at all the main locations of a company, a good contents list will go far towards dispelling the 'mumbo-jumbo' image of the old-style legal documentation for pension schemes.

One drawback is often found in the fact that trust deeds are constantly being amended, particularly for non-insured schemes, and very seldom can an absolutely current deed be produced on demand. The missing amendments should be capable of identification both by a trustee board minute and also by the issue of general notices to all current contributors and pensioners when applicable.

6.2.3.2 *The Annual Report and Accounts.* It is still surprising to find how many schemes fail to produce an Annual Report and Accounts which is distributed to all members rather than merely being made available on demand. As the law stands at present, there is no mandatory requirement for the trustees even to issue a report, although the trust deed will invariably require the accounts to be audited annually and the fund valued by the scheme actuary at stated intervals.

Fortunately, it appears from a DHSS discussion document of March 1984 that this state of affairs is likely to be remedied by future statutory enactment. The government proposals may be summarised as follows:
(1) It is intended that the trustees of all approved pension schemes will be required to make an Annual Report available to all their members within 12 months of the end of the scheme's financial year. A

statement from the scheme's actuary will be required at least once every three years.

(2) The information to be given to members should be sufficiently detailed so that an expert pension adviser could form a complete picture of the pension scheme and its financial soundness. A brief summary could also be presented in easily readable form if so wished but this would not be a legal obligation.

(3) The Annual Report should include:

    (a) The financial basis of the scheme distinguishing between funded and unfunded benefits and showing how pension increases were financed, i.e. by pre-funding or *ad hoc* by the company. Insured schemes should indicate the extent to which the life office guaranteed the benefits promised.

    (b) A set of audited accounts which should include a statement from the auditor that the contribution rate agreed by the actuary as satisfactory has been maintained.

    (c) A summary of the assets showing separately insurance policies, unit trusts, gilts, equities, debentures, convertibles, loans and properties. This would be further split into a separate list in the same categories showing individual investments which exceeded 5%, non-sterling investments and any self-investment in the parent company.

    (d) A statement of any borrowings or guarantees given.

    (e) The names of any external fund managers and their remuneration.

    (f) An actuarial statement covering the current (accrued) position and also the long-term outlook for the asset-backing and the movement in future liabilities. Brief details of the methods and assumptions used by the actuary should be shown.

These requirements would apply even to small schemes although the government appreciates that it could pose problems for them. Money purchase schemes would be exempt.

Best practice should, therefore, be to see that the Report and Accounts is drafted in a readily understandable form for all members, and to supplement it for those members in need of more assistance with a pictorial news-sheet or shortened version of the full report.

It should be acknowledged that the standard of both the full and shortened versions has shown an immense improvement over recent years and now compares favourably with the reports and accounts of many public companies.

It is also considered *good practice* to include an annual statement by the scheme actuary even if a current actuarial valuation is not available. Many schemes are now setting out the principal assumptions used by the actuary as part of the valuation report in much the same way as the notes which form part of the audited accounts. A typical example taken from the annual pension scheme report of one of the nationalised industries is shown in Appendix 6.

6.2.3.3 *Annual Benefit Statement.* This document, issued to each member, purports to show at a fixed date in each scheme year the accrued pension and lump sum benefits to which each member is entitled. It may go further and show what his present expected pension will be at normal retirement date, but since that calculation is based upon his current pensionable salary, as extended by his future years of service, it does not carry a very realistic impression. Most employees would expect to be earning more when they reach retirement date, certainly not the same figure as their current earnings, say, ten years earlier.

Nevertheless, the Annual Benefit Statement is a statement which should be produced, if only to give some reassurance as to the benefits available based on the contributions to date. It will also serve the indirect purpose of eliminating inaccuracies on the member's file. An example of a typical Annual Benefit Statement appears in Appendix 5. A separate statement showing additional voluntary contribution (AVC) benefits should also be distributed when applicable.

6.2.3.4 *General Pension Notices.* We have mentioned the problem of keeping a trust deed up to date with all previous amendments duly incorporated. So as to ensure that members are kept currently informed of these amendments which can often affect their benefit entitlement, *good practice* is to issue General Pension Notices giving outline details and for convenience to include these notices with the Annual Benefit Statement for distribution through the payroll system.

Pensions notices and pensions circulars should also be copied to any other departmental staff, e.g. personnel and wages officers.

If the numbers involved are too large, the same notices can be displayed on the usual departmental notice boards, as a suitable alternative. The helpful use of colour and good graphics design for these notices should not be underestimated.

6.2.3.5 *Audio-visual communication.* The ever-changing legislative requirements in recent years have placed a heavy communication burden on pension scheme administrators. The written word can seldom be as effective as the spoken word and when both can be combined in pictorial form, the improvement in communication is ready to hand.

The technical departments of pension consultants and consulting actuaries have responded to this demand with a plentiful supply of first-class audio-visual slide and film programmes dealing with every facet of pension scheme administration. While not inexpensive – a one-off film can cost up to £12,000 – they enable the load on the pension administrator to be spread since they can be used, without great difficulty, by personnel staff and others not familiar with the subject-matter.

Although the modern audio-visual programme is generally presented in an attractive format with graphic illustration by well-known cartoon artists to supplement actual film in full colour, and commentary by a familiar voice from the media, it is always necessary to consider the human factor in the audience. Industrial psychologists will confirm that there is a perception capacity limit on the average viewer when he is called upon to exercise his mental processes at the same time. Roughly 18/20 minutes is the maximum effective running time for any audio-visual session, with a complete break before the question-and-answer session follows on.

6.2.4 *On leaving service*

The documentation required to evidence the options available for short-term benefits, i.e. to the early leaver who is not proceeding on pension, should be strictly in accordance with the scheme rules as well as any statutory requirements such as preservation, which would also be part of the rules.

The ideal 'leaving options' document should be self-explanatory since it is very unlikely that the scheme member will have direct access to the pension department staff. It should indicate if there is any time limit to the choice of options and who should be consulted, particularly in the case of a transfer payment when the attitude or even the existence of the new scheme may not always be known at the time of withdrawal from service.

The facility of revaluation of the deferred pension should clearly show whether it is mandatory and built into the rules or permissive at the discretion of the trustees. The additional complication of providing for the compulsory revaluation of the GMP part of the scheme pension in a contracted-out scheme requires careful explanation as to the effect of franking that part of the pension against other benefits. Happily, this situation is unlikely to prevail much longer and statutory prohibition of such franking can be expected in the near future.

Having exercised his option, generally one of three – to take either a deferred pension, or a part-refund of contributions or a transfer payment to another scheme – the withdrawing member should be issued with a formal document setting out his rights under the scheme rules as they are at the time of his withdrawal. It is an important document and should be spelt out in precise but intelligible language so that the member or any of his dependants in the event of his prior decease before normal retirement date can understand to what benefits he is entitled, and that time may be many years ahead.

6.2.5 *On proceeding to pension*

Whether it is a deferred pensioner or a current employee taking his retirement – either an early, a normal or a late retirement – the same action to bring the pension into payment will generally be required. Almost every modern scheme offers the alternative of taking a substantial tax-free cash sum in commutation of part of the first pension, and it is an essential act of *good pension practice* that this option should be communicated and actioned before the retirement day is reached.

The change in financial circumstances may well be extreme and no effort should be spared by the scheme administrator to ensure that the pensioner proceeds on pension with his full entitlements. In addition, during the six months prior to retirement, the personnel department should be assisting the pensioner to apply for and obtain such other pension and supplementary benefits to which he may be entitled from the State.

Best practice is that the cash commutation payment, if chosen, and the scheme pension both become available on the first day of retirement. Unlike normal payroll or salary procedure, pensions should be paid in advance and most insured pension contracts will provide for that to be done.

The pension should be paid by cheque or credit/Giro transfer into a banking or Post Office Giro account. This ensures the maximum security and obviates the use of certificates of existence. The credit transfer should preferably be confirmed by a separate advice slip, which can be accompanied where necessary by any general pension circulars which affect pensions in payment, such as an explanation of any escalation which has been applied either by the scheme rules or by special company payment for an *ad hoc* increase.

6.3 Miscellaneous disclosure matters

The main methods of disclosing to the member his rights under the pension scheme to which he belongs have been set out above. However, there are certain specialised aspects of communication in this field which do not fall readily into the above categories. These are as follows:

6.3.1 *Rights of appeal to the trustee board*

There is an inherent right for every prospective beneficiary under a pension scheme trust deed to have access to the trustee board in the event that he has a grievance concerning any act carried out by any servant of the board. That right only applies to the benefits set out in the existing scheme rules, and cannot be extended into matters where the trust deed expressly gives the trustees a discretionary power, which is absolute and cannot be challenged.

This right should be set out in the shortened version of the rule book given to every member on joining the scheme.

6.3.2 *Powers of Pension Advisory Committees*

To provide for channels of representation on pension matters which come outside the existing scheme rules, i.e. to press for improvements or amendments, a Pension Advisory Committee is an essential feature of any sizeable company administrative structure.

The existence of these Advisory Committees should be well publicised in General Notices by the personnel departments concerned. It is not a pension department responsibility.

6.3.3 *Election of member trustees and representatives on Pension Advisory Committees*

The methods of election or selection of the member representatives on trustee boards should be well publicised by personnel departments, and subsequently the names of those member trustees when elected should be made known through the best available methods. The election of representatives to the Advisory Committees should be dealt with in the same way.

There is little point in going to the trouble of having members' representatives unless the members know who they are. This information should always be included in the Annual Report.

6.3.4 *Personal benefit advice*

This is a sensitive area for pension department staff if they are called upon to give financial advice to prospective pensioners (or their dependants) or to members on withdrawal or joining the scheme with a transfer payment.

The golden rule is to confine the advice to strictly factual information as to the benefits available and leave the decision to the member. But where problems of investment occur, such as for cash commutations or lump sum benefits, *best practice* is to make available a suitable external and independent source of advice whom you know to be reliable, possibly through your pension consultants.

There should be no charge to the member for such a service and if there are any costs they should be borne by the company and not the pension scheme.

The existence of this facility for advice should not be abused or it could prove expensive. Nevertheless, if the need arises, it should be made available and notified to prospective users by way of an individual advice by the pension department since it is monies derived from the pension fund which are at stake.

7 Member participation

Member participation in the organisational structure of pension scheme administration is now an established part of good present-day industrial relations practice.

By 'member participation' we mean direct representation of the scheme members both on the trustee board and on the Pension Advisory Committees. Both systems of representation are complementary and form the necessary counterparts of the separate pension responsibilities of the company and the trustees.

In certain nationalised industries in the public sector, the officially recognised unions may, by prior agreement, provide the member trustees, even though they may not be members of the pension scheme. It is not the intention of this chapter to enlarge upon that aspect, and we shall be concerned only with representation/participation by the members themselves in their varying capacity either as trustees or on Pension Advisory Committees.

7.1 Communication

Good communications are an essential part of member participation, and the greater part of this burden falls upon the pension scheme manager in his capacity as scheme administrator. In Chapter 6 the problems of disclosure by the company trustees and pension administrator to members were examined as they relate to the position of the following:

(1) *Non-members.* The information about pension arrangements which should be given to new employees before they actually join the pension scheme.

(2) *Current members.* The continuing flow of relevant information, rang-

ing from representation on the trustee board and Pension Advisory Committees to the more personal Annual Benefit Statement.
(3) *Pensioners.* This should cover both pensioners in payment and deferred pensioners, both of whom are still members of the pension scheme with rights protected by the trust deed and rules.

7.2 The distinction between trustee boards and Pension Advisory Committees

It is very important to grasp the essential distinction between trustee boards and Pension Advisory Committees.

7.2.1 *Trustee boards*

Trustees occupy a unique position in a pension scheme. They come between the member and his employer in all matters relating to his rights under the pension scheme.

Although the formal appointment of trustees generally originates with the company, even in the case of member trustees, nevertheless, once appointed, their main responsibility is to look after the interests of the members. The trustees are there to administer the scheme, as it then stands, and to safeguard the investments which will support the benefits promised by the trust deed and rules.

All members have an ultimate right of access to the trustees and if they feel that any of the benefits promised under the rules are being withheld, it is against the trustees and not the company that the member has his right of action under trust law.

It is no part of the trustees' duty to amend the rules unilaterally; they can only apply them as they stand.

7.2.2 *Pension Advisory Committees*

The need for Pension Advisory Committees was only properly recognised during the last decade and many employers are still reluctant to add one more level of administration.

Having reiterated the primary duties of a trustee board in the previous section, it will appear a logical development that employees should still have a more informal means of consultation relating to pension matters with their company management.

Pension Advisory Committees enable a two-way system of communication to exist between the company and employees who are members of its pension scheme. Whereas a trustee board consists of trustees, whether they represent management or the members, who are appointed to represent all members in the administration of the scheme, Pensions Advisory Committees can be set up to deal with the development of the scheme and with changes thought necessary to make it function more effectively, possibly for certain special groups of employees, and covering each participating company in a holding group.

The two-way dialogue between company and employee thus makes it possible to suggest changes in scheme benefits which can originate from either side. The cost of the improvements and the reasons for the changes can readily be brought into the discussion, which would be inappropriate for a trustee board.

The final consequence of such consultation would then be for the company management to inform the trustee board of its intention to amend the rules in accordance with the powers given under the trust deed. Any change of contribution rates which was necessary to cover an improvement of benefits would already have been cleared with the members generally by prior consultation through the Pension Advisory Committees, which is precisely the reason for their existence. Such consultation would simply not be possible through the mechanism of the trustee board.

7.3 Member participation on trustee boards

The particular functions of member participation on trustee boards can now be examined.

7.3.1 *Trustee boards*

The essential features of the pension scheme trust deed arrangements have been separately examined in Chapter 3. The role of the trustee is determined primarily by general trust law, and is subject to such special modifications of that law as are contained in the trust deed and rules of each scheme, to which the attention of each new trustee must be drawn. In particular the statutory restrictions on the investment powers of trustees are generally removed, but that does not in any way detract from the ultimate responsibility of the trustees which still remains.

All occupational pension schemes, even those with non-contributory arrangements, are required by the SFO to set up an adequate trust deed containing all the mandatory safeguard provisions (see Revenue Practice Notes 12/79 Section 22) before Revenue approval under FA 1970 is forthcoming. The new trustee, once appointed either as a management or member representative, will thereafter cease to be a representative of a particular section or class of employee. The process of establishing trustee arrangements is examined below.

7.3.2 *Selection of trustees*

While it remains true to say that the general requirements by the Revenue to set up trustee arrangements apply to all schemes, the actual structure of a trustee board can vary widely, because of the very wide range of pension scheme arrangements.

Trustees can be appointed as individual trustees but the more modern practice, especially with larger schemes, is to have a corporate trustee board to which the trustees are appointed as directors. While the SFO and OPB are prepared to accept that such trustee directors are for all practical purposes identical with sole trustees, nevertheless, steps are likely to be taken to review the law concerning pension scheme trustees.

In the case of many insured schemes it is not uncommon to find a specialised trustee company being appointed, which consists entirely of external appointees. To assist in the practical administration of the scheme and give it a more personal nature, a committee of management consisting of company representatives can be established under the trust deed.

Best practice for the trustee board is to have equal numbers of trustees drawn from management and the membership with an independent chairman, preferably of senior management or company main board status. In this way, the general membership can feel confident that the trustee board is democratic and can reach its decisions in an independent and impartial manner.

It can easily happen that many of the management trustees are also members of the pension scheme, and although their appointment will be by a separate route, their responsibilities, once appointed, are precisely the same as the member trustees.

It follows that every endeavour should be made by the chairman of the trustee board to ensure that decisions are reached by a consensus and that resort to a vote should only be as a last resort.

The appointment of the first trustees will probably have to anticipate the provisions of the trust deed or the articles of association of the corporate trustee, as the case may be. Ideally, the method of appointment/selection of the member trustees should have been settled by consultation with the members, through the aegis of the Pension Advisory Committees if they are in operation and available.

Both selection and election may be used and there would appear to be little difference in practice so far as the final outcome is concerned. It would be prudent to settle the process of the rotation of all trustees including the member trustees at the same time.

The method of rotation, selection and removal of trustees should have regard to the practical difficulty if continuity of trustee administration is to be achieved and it can then be embodied in the formal legal documents.

Best practice is to have written into the rules the requirement that member trustees should be contributing members of the pension scheme, and should cease to be eligible when no longer in the employment.

7.3.3 *Training of trustees*

Special attention must be paid to the training of all trustees, both management and member representatives, in the proper discharge of their duties, and this again places a heavy responsibility on the pension scheme manager. It has already been pointed out that the trust deed together with the rules is the basic document on which rest the entire rights and obligations of the company, the trustees and the members. It follows that this documentation must be clear and easily comprehended by the trustees.

Once appointed, further training both in-house and on external courses should be used wherever possible, including informal visits to all the schemes' professional advisers and any external investment managers. The more knowledgeable the new trustees become, the more efficient will be the discharge of their trustee responsibilities.

7.3.4 *Trustee board sub-committees*

Most trustee boards (or their committees of management) of any sizeable pension scheme will have so much routine work involved in scheme administration and the supervision of the investments that it will be necessary (under the powers given by the trust deed) to set up sub-committees to deal with the following separate parts of their activities:
(1) Investment (share portfolio).
(2) Investment (property).
(3) Audit and accounts.
(4) Alternative investments (for preliminary investigation of new types of investment).
(5) Discretionary payments of death benefits (usually *ad hoc* for any non-straightforward case).

These sub-committees can only draw their delegated powers from the trustee board under the provisions of the trust deed. Thus, they can never usurp the responsibilities of the main trustee board, and this particularly applies to their investment functions whether these are carried out by in-house staff or external investment fund managers.

It has sometimes been said that the trustees are only responsible for the appointment of good investment fund managers – but not for the manner in which those managers carry out their responsibilities. In fact, this is not true, and reference to the judgement in the case of *Evans* v. *London Co-op Retail Society* (1976) will show how the trustees continue to hold the ultimate responsibility for ensuring that the investments are properly controlled, with the object of securing the members' benefits. Recent American legislation, the Employee Retirement Income Security Act 1974 and the Tax Equity and Fiscal Responsibility Act 1982, has reduced this aspect into a very clear and very burdensome statutory form.

7.4 The relationship of trustees with advisers and staff

The relationship of trustees with the following will be examined in this section:

(1) The professional advisers to the scheme.
(2) Externally appointed and in-house investment fund managers.
(3) Pension department staff.

7.4.1 Relationship with professional advisers

All the professional advisers should be appointed by the trustee board and the appointments should be reviewed periodically, preferably at the time when the Annual Report and Accounts is being approved.

A formal letter of appointment should always be issued, setting out in reasonably general detail the guidelines for the matters on which the adviser gives advice. It should be noted that it is a one-way directional flow and in no way should professional advisers be called upon to exercise any delegated powers.

The trust deed should provide for the remuneration of advisers, but, unlike the private trust, with a charging clause allowing for the remuneration of trustees in their professional capacity, the pension fund trustee should never allow himself to adopt an anomalous role and be paid for his services.

If the trustee board feel unable to accept the advice of a professional adviser, they are perfectly entitled not to do so, but it should be on good and certain grounds.

7.4.2 Relationship with investment fund managers

Externally appointed investment fund managers and in-house fund managers are in the same position with regard to the trustee board. Their operations should be set out precisely in a formal letter of appointment indicating the clear lines of demarcation beyond which their discretionary power no longer holds good.

Whereas the other professional advisers' responsibility is to advise the trustees, the external investment fund manager has the additional function of management, albeit in a delegated form, but it can easily become a very wide type of discretionary investment management after the various exclusions have been taken into account. For that reason alone a much more frequent form of control should be exercised by the trustee board who retain the ultimate responsibility. One form of this control is by way of an independent fund performance measurement service as shown in Chapter 11.

7.4.3 Relationship with pension department staff

This is a matter not normally given the proper consideration due to its importance. It may often happen that the pension scheme manager is also a member of the trustee board, especially in the larger schemes in the private sector. The same problem of a conflict of interest may arise in the case of any other management nominated trustee.

A heavy responsibility lies on the pension scheme manager to ensure that a proper balance is achieved in his relationship with the trustees. The trustees are entitled to full information not merely on matters requiring their decision, but on any matter which may have a bearing on the proper performance of their duties, especially changes in statute law, the exercise of their discretionary powers as to benefits, and the state of the investment portfolio.

A more tactful approach may be needed when a member or management trustee makes enquiries as to the records of individual scheme members, which are not specifically concerned with the pension benefits, but are for some other, undisclosed purpose. The pension scheme manager in his own position has an obligation to preserve the confidentiality of his records, for which he is responsible to his employer and the company management.

8 Actuarial valuations

The true cost of a pension scheme cannot be determined until the last member has retired, drawn his pension and died. The cost depends upon who joins the scheme, how long they remain in employment, what benefits they receive and how long they live.

There are different ways of meeting the cost of pension benefits. At one extreme, the benefits can be paid by the company as they fall due. This is the 'pay-as-you-go' system, where no pension fund is built up. At the other extreme, it would be possible, in theory, for the whole cost of an employee's pension to be met on the day he started work. The vast majority of UK pension schemes are funded by an intermediate method which aims to spread the cost over the employee's working career, so that his benefits are fully funded by the time he retires.

8.1 Main reasons for external funding

The important points to consider can be summarised under the headings of security, prudence, equity and stability:

8.1.1 Security

If the payment of pension benefits is to be more than just a promise, the employer and, of course, the prospective beneficiaries will wish to ensure that the rights of the beneficiaries are secured and safeguarded as they accrue, and that cash will be readily available when required for the payment of benefits. The accumulation of assets held in trust for the benefit of members, the assets being outside the control of the employer and with a value not dependent on the employer's future prosperity or even his continued existence, is regarded as the best way of achieving the desired security.

8.1.2 *Prudence*

An employer will wish to know the estimated long-term cost of his pension arrangements. He should certainly be aware of this either when pricing the goods and services he offers or in assessing their profitability. In this connection the current pension outgo on a pay-as-you-go basis may be a totally inadequate guide to the long-term cost of the pension scheme.

8.1.3 *Equity*

This means equity between generations of employees. It is argued that in the private sector at least, the cost of an employee's pension rights should be charged against the profits which he has helped to generate, so that each generation pays for its own pensions. This implies the setting aside of assets in respect of future liabilities – that is, advance provision in the form of an accumulation of assets.

8.1.4 *Stability*

The employer will normally wish the burden of pension costs to fall evenly from year to year (e.g. as a level percentage of payroll). This does not mean that the cost in terms of benefit outgo will be constant but that the contribution input as a percentage of salary is stable. A fund into which contributions can be paid facilitates this aim.

8.1.5 *Flexibility*

An external fund can also, of course, afford the employer a reasonable degree of flexibility if he wishes periodically to vary his contribution in times of particular difficulty or prosperity.

8.2 Different funding methods

In determining and recommending a suitable level of contribution, actuaries may employ different funding methods having regard to the objectives of the employer and the trustees. The employer may wish to pay more now and less later or vice versa. Actual levels of contribution reflect the so-called 'pace of funding'.

There are several possibilities of which the two most popular are as follows:

8.2.1 *Aggregate funding*

This is generally the method most popular with schemes which are not insured. Cost estimates are based on employees' service to retirement and anticipated salaries at retirement and these cost estimates are converted to a contribution rate normally expressed as a level percentage of payroll which, if the actuarial assumptions are borne out in practice, can be expected to remain stable over the long term. If the actuarial assumptions are 'correct', payment of this level of contribution will be sufficient to provide the emerging benefits in respect of all members over the period until the last beneficiary has drawn his or her last benefit payment.

8.2.2 *Discontinuance funding*

This method is adopted in respect of some insured schemes. Under this method, projections are made for a defined control period (e.g. 5 years or 20 years). Cost estimates are based on service to the end of the projection period and anticipated salaries at the end of the projection period. The objective is to provide emerging benefits over the control period and to provide withdrawal or discontinuance benefits in respect of employees still in service at the end of the period. This method generally results in lower contribution rates initially, i.e. a slower pace of funding.

This method has had to be modified for contracted-out schemes since it is necessary to allow for the escalation of GMPs up to retirement.

8.3 The purpose of actuarial valuations

In order to make advance financial provision under whichever funding method is adopted, it is necessary to estimate what the cost of benefits will turn out to be. This is done in an actuarial valuation. The actuary estimates this cost by making assumptions about future events and trends. These assumptions do not affect the true cost of the scheme, only the rate at which money is set aside to meet that cost.

8.4 Valuation assumptions

In order to make his estimates of the future cost of benefits, the actuary must make a wide range of assumptions about the future course of events. The assumptions can be split into two categories as follows:

(1) *Demographic.* This category includes mortality rates before and after retirement, turnover rates and rates of early retirement due to ill-health. Standard mortality tables are generally used. It is important not to underestimate how long pensioners will live. Mortality rates are generally very stable, particularly in large schemes, and can be predicted fairly accurately. The death of a member does not necessarily strain the finances of a fund because the death benefit payment is balanced by the fact that no pension will be payable.

(2) *Financial.* This category includes the rate of investment return, rates of future salary increases and, where appropriate, rates of future pension increases. These are much harder to predict accurately. They tend to fluctuate quite sharply, particularly when rates of inflation are volatile. Fortunately, however, over the long term they tend to move in step.

The key factor is the relationship between the assumed rate of return and the other financial assumptions. The gap between them is often referred to as the 'real rate of return', but it is important to be clear as to whether the rate of return is being compared with the rate of increase in prices or salaries and wages. It is customary at the present time to assume positive real rates of return, but on a cautious basis.

There is a range of assumptions which most actuaries would regard as acceptable. If relatively optimistic assumptions are chosen, the valuation will result in a lower contribution rate (or a larger surplus or a smaller deficiency) than if relatively pessimistic assumptions are adopted.

If the optimistic assumptions turn out to have been too optimistic, the contribution rate will have to be increased (or the surplus will have changed into a deficiency) later on.

The actuary reviews his assumptions at each valuation. To do this, he compares his previous assumptions with what has actually happened and then, in the light of current economic conditions, decides whether or not to alter his assumptions.

It is now common practice with large schemes for the actuary, before making a final decision, to discuss his assumptions (particularly the financial ones) with the trustees and the employer, since the provision for pensions is recognised as part of the overall financial planning of the business. A specimen set of valuation assumptions which would form part of the actuarial report to the trustees is shown as Appendix 6.

Valuations should be carried out fairly frequently (usually every three years) so that any under- or over-funding resulting from the assumptions made at the previous valuation not being borne out in practice can be detected before the position becomes serious.

8.5 The valuation process

The actual process by which the actuary arrives at the result of his valuation tends to be regarded as a mystery by the layman. Before the actuary can commence work he requires a great deal of information as follows:

(1) *Membership data.* Individual details of the membership of the scheme (current, retired and deferred members) are presented to the actuary, who normally subjects the data to a wide range of checks on their accuracy. He also requires details of all members who have died or left the scheme over the period since his previous valuation in order to test the actual experience against his assumptions.

(2) *Investment data.* The actuary requires details of the assets of the scheme, including accounts for the period since the last valuation, and a list of investments at the valuation date.

Actuarial calculations are based on the theory of probabilities and the theory of compound interest (or discounted cash flow) and it may be of assistance to give an explanation of the significance and working of these theories. They are an essential element in the proper understanding of an actuarial valuation of a pension fund.

8.6 Calculation of present value of liabilities

The association of a survival probability and a rate of discount lies at the root of the actuary's technique of arriving at a 'present value'. Ideally, the actuary turns to statistics of the experience of a class of lives identical in material character to the members of the scheme. He then determines from these statistics the probability that each individual will survive to receive each future annual payment, multiplies this by the appropriate amount of the payment and discounts to allow for the rate of interest to the present time. By applying this technique to each future payment and summing the results, he produces an overall total which gives the amount of the benefit liabilities. The probability of survival can be calculated, where appropriate, to allow not only for mortality, but also for such factors as withdrawal from service and early retirement for reasons of ill-health.

The same technique is applied to arrive at the present value of the future contributions to be paid to the fund by both employer and the members.

8.6.1 *Presentation*

The liabilities are valued by collecting together the discounted values of future benefits. The present value of the liabilities is compared with the value of the fund and the present value of the future contributions. (See Fig. 3.)

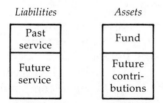

Fig. 3 Valuation balance sheet.

8.6.2 *Optimum Contribution Rate*

Normally, total liabilities for past and future service are compared with total assets. The actuary recommends a contribution rate to produce equality. Sometimes, the result is shown by assuming that the existing contribution rate will continue and calculating the surplus of assets over liabilities, or deficiency. In certain circumstances, the valuation may simply consist of a comparison between the liabilities for past service and the amount of the fund.

8.7 Actuarial valuation of fund investments

Pension fund accounts normally show both the historic cost and the market values of the fund's investments. Neither of these figures is particularly suitable for an actuarial valuation to assess the long-term funding rate for a pension scheme. Historic costs are of little or no interest to the actuary and market values fluctuate too sharply. Various methods have been developed by actuaries aimed at identifying an underlying long-term value of the investments which remains relatively stable from one valuation to the next.

8.7.1 *The 'discounted cash flow' (DCF) technique*

In determining the value at which the assets of a pension scheme should be brought into the valuation balance sheet, the actuary is primarily concerned with the future flow of income which is expected from those assets. In this context, income includes realised capital appreciation as well as interest and dividends. A logical method of placing a value on the flow of future income is, therefore, to calculate the discounted present value by the same general technique as is applied to value the liabilities of the fund and the future contributions. In this process, the rate of interest employed for discount purposes would be the same rate of interest as is used for discounting the other items in the balance sheet.

8.7.2 *DCF value of fixed interest securities and equities*

So far as fixed interest securities are concerned, this can be a simple process of discounting the future fixed interest payments and adding the discounted value of the redemption amount when the stock matures. For an irredeemable fixed interest stock, the value would be the annual interest divided by the valuation rate of interest. The valuation of equity shares presents a more complex problem since the current market yield and the anticipated future potential for dividend growth will vary substantially between individual shares. In practice, the actuary would probably presume the same annual compound rate of growth in dividends in respect of the whole equity portfolio.

8.7.3 *An examination of DCF technique*

It can be difficult to apply this 'discounted cash flow' approach to property investments and these assets, particularly if they represent only a small proportion of the total fund, would often be taken at their estimated market value. Amounts of cash would similarly be taken at their face value.

This method of valuing assets had become widely employed before interest rates rose sharply in the late 1970s. Actuaries have, however, encountered the problem that discounting the expected interest and capital proceeds from fixed interest stocks at the valuation rate of interest can produce values for these assets very considerably in excess of their market values.

This method of valuing the assets essentially capitalises the future investment profits expected from fixed interest holdings, and many actuaries now feel it prudent to reduce the extent to which this interest surplus is allowed to emerge at a single valuation. It is, therefore, becoming more usual to value the fixed interest part of an asset portfolio in a way consistent in relation to market values with the corresponding values placed on other assets.

8.7.4 *An alternative method of valuing assets*

This approach can in fact be generalised by valuing all of the assets of a pension fund as if they were equity assets matching a particular index, usually the FT Actuaries' All-Share Index, and valuing this notional portfolio on a specified yield basis. The difference between the specified yield basis and the valuation rate of interest would represent approximately the allowance for future dividend growth.

Thus, if the actuary's valuation rate of interest is 8% per annum, and the yield basis chosen for valuing the notional portfolio matching the FT Actuaries' All-Share Index is $5\frac{1}{2}$% per annum, the implicit allowance for the future dividend growth would be approximately $2\frac{1}{2}$% per annum.

If at the date of the valuation the actual gross yield on the FT Actuaries' All-Share Index were 6%, then this method of valuation would produce a higher value than a market value. If alternatively the actual yield on the FT Actuaries' All-Share Index were 5%, the above method of valuation would produce a lower value than market value.

It will be apparent from the above discussion that the method of valuing assets by discounting future receipts must be treated with caution. For this reason, some actuaries have preferred to revert to taking the market value of assets as a reasonable guide but, in order to avoid giving too much effect to short-term fluctuations, to calculate an average market value over, say, a two- or three-year period.

8.8 Analysis of surplus

As mentioned earlier in this chapter, the actuary will, in connection with the periodic valuation of a pension scheme, compare his former valuation assumptions with the actual experience of the scheme over the intervaluation period. This analysis of the experience is an essential tool assisting the actuary to carry out an analysis of the surplus (or deficiency) which has arisen over that period on the assumption that contribution rates remain unchanged. Although there may be very little overall difference between the valuation result and that of the previous valuation, the result would nevertheless represent the net effect of a number of interacting factors, some of which will have given rise to a valuation profit and others to a valuation strain.

An analysis of the surplus into items such as investment profits, salary strain and the effects of new entrants and withdrawals will provide a valuable check to the actuary on the result of his valuation. It will also be of interest to the employer, the trustees and the members of the scheme in helping them to understand the way in which the fund is progressing.

8.9 The actuary's report

Because actuarial calculations are not easily understood by most laymen, it is important that the written report of the actuary should be fully comprehensible to all those concerned with the pension scheme.

The report will normally be a substantial document and would completely review the position since the last report was issued.

8.9.1 Introductory section

An introductory section should remind the reader of the result of the last valuation and any recommendations which accompanied it. It would recite any changes made to the rules of the scheme in the light of these recommendations or for other reasons (e.g. in response to legislation).

8.9.2 Data

The report will describe the data submitted to the actuary and the manner in which they were submitted, e.g. on computer tape, schedules or handwritten cards. Appendixes to the report would normally give detailed summaries of membership, classified by sex and type of member, and would compare these details with those of the last valuation.

8.9.3 Reference to the latest audited accounts

The report might also include a summary of information from the audited accounts of the scheme, which in the past was often limited to a recital of the running yields achieved in each year since the last valuation, but which might now include a more detailed schedule of investment performance measurement figures. The report should show a breakdown of the assets of the fund at the valuation date, indicating the book value, market value and the value adopted for the valuation.

8.9.4 Analysis of intervaluation experience

There would then be a summary and discussion of the analysis made of the experience of the scheme over the intervaluation period, and each item of the valuation basis would be considered in turn. Separate sections of the report would consider the demographic assumptions, such as mortality, withdrawals and premature retirements, and the financial assumptions, such as the valuation rate of interest, the allowance for salary increases and the allowance, if any, for increases in pensions, either in deferment or in payment.

8.9.5 *Valuation of assets and presentation of results*

Finally, there would be a section on the valuation of the assets of the scheme, followed by a presentation of the results of the valuation in the form of a valuation balance sheet. The report may include a brief summary of the analysis of surplus or deficiency.

8.9.6 *Consideration of any recommended changes to contribution rate*

Since the principal purpose of the report is normally to assess whether any change is necessary to the employer's rate of contribution to the fund, this would normally be the main item covered by the section dealing with the recommendations to the trustees and/or the company.

If the result of the valuation were to reveal a balance of liability on the assumption that contributions remained unchanged, then the actuary would have to recommend some increase in contributions or, alternatively, some cutback in the benefits of the scheme.

If the valuation revealed a surplus, the report could discuss the alternatives of either reducing future contributions or considering various improvements in benefits.

8.9.7 *Principal actuarial assumptions used in valuation*

It is now common practice to include as part of the actuaries' report a summary of the principal assumptions employed in the actuarial calculations. An example of such a summary is shown in Appendix 6.

8.10 Alternative 'discontinuance' basis of valuation

It has become more common for valuation reports to include a subsidiary section indicating the result of an alternative valuation carried out on a 'discontinuance' basis. This would show the position of the fund in the event of an immediate winding-up as at the valuation date. It would, therefore, compare the value of accrued liabilities (calculated in accordance with the scheme's winding-up provisions and *normally with no provision for future salary increases*) with the *market value of the assets* at that date.

9 Company takeovers and pension scheme mergers

This chapter will consider the problems concerning the transfer of pension benefits which arise when a company is taken over by way of purchase of its shareholdings or part of an existing company is sold off.

The three familiar situations are as follows:

(1) *The takeover bid*. The most common is when a bid is made for the issued share capital of an existing company with a separate pension scheme of its own.

In such a situation it is unlikely there will be a separate vending agreement and the transferring employees may derive little or no protection for their pension rights from the offer documents other than a general statement from the purchasers that existing pension rights will be honoured and continued.

There is thus no immediate urgency to spell out any further safeguards, but inevitably the question of merging with the purchaser company's scheme will arise, if it is their normal practice to centralise pension arrangements.

(2) *Part-sale of a business*. More difficult is the situation where part of an existing company, possibly a complete subsidiary, is sold off.

Generally, in such cases, there is a considerable amount of negotiation concerning the commercial aspects and the price which will permit the opportunity for safeguarding personnel matters such as continuing employment and pension rights on transfer.

These matters will form part of the vending agreement, and the manner in which pension rights are dealt with is set out later in this chapter.

(3) *Pension scheme mergers*. Following upon either an offer to purchase or

the partial sale of a company, the question of merging the pension arrangements of the incoming employees with the existing pension schemes will undoubtedly arise. The technical processes involved in scheme mergers will be dealt with later in this chapter.

9.1 Individual early leavers and small groups of employees

The position of individual early leavers or small groups of employees not forming part of a complete participating company who are thrown up by such takeovers is not covered in this chapter. Their rights and entitlements on leaving service, whether or not they agree to transfer to the new employer, will normally be determined by the rules of their original scheme.

There is some justification, dependent always upon the wording of the trust deed and the discretion given to the trustees, for providing for a transfer of the full actuarial reserve in cases where an identifiable group of employees is transferred. The forthcoming legislation promised in 1984 to dynamise paid-up pensions – and thus ensure a more realistic transfer value – will go a long way towards meeting this problem.

Where there is to be an offer of continuing employment, the statutory rights of the transferring employees are covered by the Employment Protection (Consolidation) Act 1978 and the later Transfer of Employments Act 1981. These Acts specifically exclude occupational pension rights and it is, therefore, important that, where at all possible these should be protected in the vending agreement. A suitable clause would read:

The purchaser shall undertake all liability in respect of such employees as from the completion date and shall take all steps necessary to secure continuity of the existing pension and life assurance arrangements . . . (but without prejudice to the generality of the foregoing will set up a pension and life assurance scheme for the transferring staff on the lines outlined in the attached booklets of their existing scheme).

All these points should be covered when drafting the relevant covenants in the vending agreement so that the transferring employees' pension expectations will not be prejudiced and claims for constructive dismissal and loss of pension rights are avoided.

9.2 The vending agreement – part-sale of undertaking

9.2.1 Responsibilities of vendor

In the case of a vending agreement, the responsibility for ensuring the protection of the pension rights of the transferring employees falls primarily upon the vendor company. Reference will have to be made to the following documentation in both schemes in order that the pension rights can be effectively transferred:

(1) The trust deed and rules of both schemes, or the benefit structure of the proposed scheme if the purchaser has not a suitable scheme available.
(2) The preservation requirements of SSA 1973 and the question of the continuation of the vendor's own pension scheme.
(3) The contracting-out provisions of SSPA 1975 in so far as they relate to the GMP and the short-term benefit options available to both the employer and the member.
(4) The responsibility for meeting any shortfall in the sum required to ensure the continuation of past service rights on the same basis, in the incoming scheme, and how that cost shall be met.

9.2.2 *Responsibility of legal adviser*

It is imperative that the vendor's legal adviser should keep in close touch with the pension scheme manager in order to ensure that the financial cost of transferring the accrued pension benefits and the continuation of the guaranteed scale of benefits in the purchaser's employment does not cause the commercial negotiations to founder.

There are recent cases, particularly in the public sector, where the unfunded liability of the pension scheme has nearly exceeded the purchase price, and the burden of meeting that shortfall had to be passed to a third party, namely the taxpayer.

Having determined from an examination of the relevant clauses in both trust deeds that a transfer payment is both possible and acceptable, the legal adviser will next be concerned with the amount to be provided in the event of any shortfall in the transfer value payment.

The onus for determining the amount of any shortfall will normally rest with the actuary of the purchaser's scheme (after consultation with the actuary of the outgoing scheme). The allocation of the shortfall payment, if any, should be covered by a suitable covenant, which may involve an abatement of the purchase price, if the burden is to remain with the vendor.

The purchaser may not have a suitable scheme readily available, and in such cases it may be necessary for the vendor with the consent of the SFO to allow the transferring employees to remain in their old scheme until suitable alternative arrangements have been made, as indicated in the draft covenant clause above. The SFO is very flexible and generally allows up to two years for the necessary alternative arrangements to be set up. During that period the purchaser company (as the new employer) will be required to become a participating company in the vendor's scheme in order to obtain the necessary statutory consent for treatment of contributions as allowable expenses.

9.2.3 *Actuarial matters*

Under a vending agreement which only requires the determination of the correct transfer payment covering the pension benefits and not the transfer of the entire fund, the actuarial problems revolve mainly around the assumptions applied to both schemes and the valuation of the relative scales of benefit to determine if there is any shortfall. It is of considerable help if both schemes are contracted out and they have a common basis of valuing the preserved GMP.

The vendor's actuary will naturally have regard to the wording of the trust deed before advising the trustees as to the amount of the transfer payment. And he will consult with the purchaser's actuary as to the basis on which his funding assumptions are made, before advising the vendor as to the amount of any shortfall resulting from any guarantee if continuing benefit entitlement is given to the transferring employees.

9.2.4 *Pension scheme manager's responsibilities*

The scheme manager or administrator will bear the main burden of co-ordinating the action necessary for the proper drafting of the relevant clauses in the vending agreement. A checklist is given in 9.2.5 below.

One aspect which is sometimes difficult to cover in a vending situation is the question of communication and the disclosure of all relevant facts to the transferring employees. Because of the confidential nature of the commercial negotiations, it is not always possible for pension matters to be disclosed in advance of completion date and the responsibility of anticipating any difficulties in these matters rests firmly with the scheme manager or administrator. Where there is to be a continuing employment, albeit with a change in the name of the employer, pensions are excluded from statutory protection and rest upon the rules of the existing scheme, unlike the remaining matters in the employees' contracts of employment.

Nevertheless, there will still be many takeover situations where the question of transferring pension rights will be very much an *ex post facto* matter.

9.2.5 *Vending agreement checklist*

While this checklist is primarily meant for the use of the vendor's professional advisers and pension staff, it will also be of help to the prospective purchaser in order that he can be made aware of the financial implications of the transfer of employees' pension benefits. The following actions should be taken by the vendor's scheme manager before sale:

(1) Check the purchaser company's pension scheme documentation and determine contracting-out status under SSPA 1975.
(2) Ensure that the vendor's trust deed permits the transfer of the full

actuarial reserve for the group of employees being transferred, or ascertain that the trustees have to make a specific exercise of their discretion in that respect.

(3) Examine the trust deed of the purchaser company to determine whether it has the necessary powers to receive a transfer value and convert the payment into additional added years credit or only a paid-up pension. If there is any doubt, a specific covenant should be required from the purchaser in order to provide enforceable rights for the transferring employees.

(4) If possible, have both sets of consulting actuaries put in touch with each other to ascertain the basic funding assumptions they apply to the separate schemes, so that the comparison of benefits can logically be determined.

(5) Draft covenant clauses in the vending agreement to ascertain where the liability falls for covering the financial cost in meeting any shortfall in the corresponding pension benefits to be provided by the incoming scheme, and if it is to be met by way of offset against the purchase price.

(6) Settle the level of pension benefit it is desired to achieve. *Good practice* would normally give full equated years credit in the purchaser's scheme, so that effectively there is no loss of pension rights. The cost of such an undertaking is difficult to define within the pre-sale timetable and may not precisely be known until the consulting actuaries have made their calculations with all the necessary individual membership information available.

(7) Prepare draft announcements for notifying the transferring staff of the steps which are being taken to protect their accrued and future pension benefits. It is very helpful if the announcement can refer to the necessary assurances covered by the covenants given by the purchaser in the vending agreement. The purchaser company should be responsible for issuing their own literature to the incoming staff so as to avoid any possibility of confusion which may result from joint documentation.

(8) Having regard to the progress of the commercial negotiations, hold meetings of Pension Advisory Committees when the terms of the transfer of pension rights have been agreed in principle. It would be commercially improper to make them the subject of negotiation and the onus lies on the pension scheme manager to obtain the optimum transfer terms within the commercial constraints imposed.

9.3 Mergers of pension schemes

It has been pointed out above that in practice the most common takeover situation which will face the company secretary is the purchase of the issued share capital of a company, either by agreement or through a published bid for the shares in the open market. In such a situation, it is unusual to find any specific reference to pension rights other than a general reassurance in the offer documents, such as: 'That it is the intention to expand/retain the present business with its existing management and staff. Full protection will be given to the pension rights of existing employees'. Very seldom will any more specific statements appear unless the unions have been brought into the takeover battle. Indeed, it would only add an unnecessary complication to go any further with regard to employment matters at a time when the main objective is to convince the existing shareholders that an attractive price is being offered for their shares and the voting rights they carry.

This may appear to be a case of putting off the day of reckoning, but since most private sector pension schemes are unique, it is by no means certain that the benefits of the purchaser company's existing scheme are superior to those of the company which has been taken over. No action is therefore required at the date when the takeover succeeds, and the existing employees' contracts of employment, including membership of their own pension scheme, will proceed undisturbed.

Practical difficulties will inevitably arise when the employments become integrated and the problems of pay/salary patterns with differential pension benefits has to be recognised. Even if the takeover company is operated as a separate undertaking or division, sooner or later the question of staff transfers will arise and the problem of parallel pension schemes will have to be settled, no matter how much it is played down initially.

Good practice is to start actuarial assessments of the parallel schemes as soon as the takeover is completed, without giving any undertaking or statement as to the intentions of the company management until the full facts are known and the financial implications costed out. The commercial considerations will still be paramount at that stage so that a viable undertaking still exists to be able to offer continuing employment to the workforce.

One other step will normally be necessary at this stage, that is to confirm the appointment of the existing trustees of the takeover scheme, or to appoint new trustees, as is generally the case. The situation with regard to the staff of the incoming scheme pension department is different: they should be integrated immediately with the staff of the merger company, both to ensure continuity and, equally important, to rationalise discretionary procedures.

In the checklist for merger situations (9.3.4) note has been made of the importance of distinguishing any pension commitment brought in with the takeover company which may not be a liability of the formal pension scheme. Supplementary pensions and augmentation are areas where a good deal of discretion may have been applied. Sickness and permanent disability pensions are also matters needing urgent identification so that the actual liabilities of the incoming scheme can be identified.

Generally, augmentation of pensions is the financial liability of the principal company and this may well have an effect on the trading figures if it had not been disclosed.

Many of the matters already discussed under the heading 'The vending agreement – part-sale of undertaking' will also apply to the residual problem of merging two pension schemes following a takeover. The responsibilities of the professional advisers and the pension scheme manager will be examined below. Again, the main burden will fall on the pension scheme manager to co-ordinate the personnel and industrial relations aspects as well as those of the pensions department.

9.3.1 *Legal matters*

9.3.1.1 *Trust deed and rules.* An examination of the two sets of trust deeds and rules will show what can be done to secure an equitable treatment of pension benefits for the transferring employees. Essentially, there should be a specific sub-clause under the priorities rule in the main trust deed dealing with the transfer of the pension scheme and the treatment of both the liabilities and the underlying assets in the circumstances described. If there is no such clause, the trustees of the incoming scheme should be asked by the principal company to make the necessary alteration. The same process should be applied to the trust deed of the merger company.

What is more difficult to amend is the clause, still commonly found and dating back to the early 1960s when nationalisation fears were widespread, setting down built-in rights for the scheme members in the event of a takeover. Such a clause could require, for example, specific majorities of scheme members, possibly present in person, in favour of any alterations involving pension benefits following a merger.

9.3.1.2 *Closure resolutions.* Assuming that the areas of difficulty mentioned above have been dealt with, the necessary resolutions will have to be drafted for the two trustee boards, the one to close down their scheme and the other to accept the liabilities of the incoming members on the defined basis set out in the announcement literature.

9.3.1.3 *Transfer of assets.* The transfer of the underlying assets is a responsibility of the pension scheme/fund manager, but care should be taken to ensure that the transfer of any securities proceeds under a nominal and not an *ad valorem* stamp duty, as being between two trustee holders and with the same beneficiary. The actual transfer of the securities should be carefully checked and controlled whether it is to new fund managers or to your own investment manager.

9.3.1.4 *Transfer of membership.* A final but important matter is the drafting of the complicated 'Form of application for transfer and entry into the new merged pension scheme'. This is in itself a contractual document addressed to both the two employer companies and the two trustee boards. An example of a form of application for transfer is given as Appendix 7.

Each stage of the transfer process must be clearly set out in the following way:
(1) *The application to join the new pension scheme.* This can be in the normal pattern and effectively it provides the consideration at law to enable the transfer document to have the necessary validity. It will also carry the normal obligation to pay contributions and to abide by the rules of the new scheme.
(2) *A form of proxy.* Where there is a clause in the discontinuing pension scheme requiring the consent of the members either present in person or by proxy, a form of proxy incorporating the resolutions is necessary. This should indicate the position and entitlements of any dissentient minority which should previously have been set out in the announcement literature.
(3) *Form of agreement.* With recitals and following on from the application in (1) above, this sets out the agreement of the member to the transfer by his old trustee of the underlying assets in his old scheme to the trustees of the new scheme, thereby authorising his old trustees to release those assets and to take such amending action as is necessary to make changes in the scheme rules to put the transfer into effect. Thenceforth, the old trustees are released from any liability in respect of such transferred assets.
(4) *Notice of intention to transfer to (another) contracted-out scheme.* If there is a transfer from a non-contracted-out scheme to another non-contracted-out scheme, no further action is required. Generally, however, this complication exists and since the majority of private-sector pension schemes are contracted out, it is necessary to issue a formal notification in the circumstances we are discussing.

   Previously, three months' prior notification was required before the new merger pension arrangements could come into effect, but the OPB no longer insist on that period, merely requiring that the notification should be communicated and recorded. A suitable place for recording is on the reverse of the application form.

9.3.2 *Actuarial matters*

The task of the actuaries in a merger situation is more delicate than in a part-sale, where the main responsibility is to evaluate the transferring liabilities and determine the amount of the transfer value available for the transferring members to cover those liabilities.

9.3.2.1 *Measuring cost of comparative benefits*. In a merger situation, the transferring members are all still in the same employment and, save for the provision for any dissentients, all the scheme assets are being transferred. The main task is to ensure that there is no disparity of benefits between the old members and the new merging members for similar periods of service. Before that can be done, the respective costs of the liability under the old and under the new schemes has to be established and agreed between the actuaries of both schemes, and a check made that the termination clause of the taken-over scheme will allow for the proposed merger.

It is seldom that any two self-administered schemes in the private sector will have exactly the same benefits and contribution levels and use the same funding assumptions.

9.3.2.2 *Benefit structure of new scheme*. Once the takeover is completed, *best practice* is to endeavour to secure prior agreement between the two managements as to the scale of benefit to be given to the new members from the incoming company scheme. The problem is greatly simplified if full equated years in the merger scheme can be offered, with an over-riding guarantee for a strictly limited period of, say, five years to cover any anomalies such as sometimes occurred under high accrual rates in the older type of money purchase schemes.

9.3.2.3 *Value of transferred assets*. That ideal solution may, however, carry cost implications. Still, it has the advantage that it reduces the area of possible disagreement between the two sets of actuaries. The incoming scheme assets taken at their market or cost value can readily be measured as from merger date and the costing of the improved liability in the merged scheme will be determined on the existing assumptions used by that scheme.

9.3.2.4 *Procedure for dealing with actuarial deficiency*. While the area of actuarial disagreement may be reduced, there still remains the eventual reconciliation of the transferred assets with the cost of providing the uplifted benefits in the merged scheme. If these cancel out, it would be very unusual: there is usually either a surplus or a deficiency. Provided prior agreement has been reached as to the scale of benefit to be provided, any deficiency cost will be a matter of financial adjustment between the two managements, with the incoming company generally carrying the charge.

9.3.2.5 *Disposal of surplus*. The question of any surplus over and above the amount required to provide the uplifted benefits must always be anticipated and a suitable assurance given in the announcement literature in order to reassure the transferring members that they are not to be deprived of any further improvement to benefits which might thereby be possible. (The trust deed is not generally of specific help in this area.) This question is examined more fully in 9.3.3 below. The actuary's responsibility will be to evaluate the surplus in the terms of the improved benefits.

9.3.3 *Pension scheme manager's responsibilities*

The co-ordination of the merger process generally rests with the pension scheme manager or administrator: he has to both initiate and follow through to a successful conclusion. Normally there should be sufficient time to enable the personnel department to take adequate action in the industrial relations field parallel to the preparation of the covering legal documentation by the pensions department. The two lines of action must proceed in parallel to achieve the intended result.

9.3.3.1 *Merger checklist.* The detailed requirements for the merger checklist are shown in 9.3.4 below. Reference has already been made to the examination of the powers given under the two sets of trust deeds and legal advice should always be taken to secure any necessary amendments to those powers so as to facilitate the merger process.

9.3.3.2 *Form of application to transfer.* Likewise, the importance of the proper drafting of the 'Form of application for admission' to the new merged scheme has been emphasised. The remaining responsibility of the pension scheme manager is to prepare adequate announcement literature to follow on with the consultative arrangements made by the personnel departments and the legal documentation necessary to complete the merger process.

9.3.3.3 *Consultation with members and Pension Advisory Committees.* If there is already a Pension Advisory/Consultative Committee structure available, the consultation will obviously start through that channel. But a merger situation will normally require full meetings to which all the transferring staff should be invited so as to ensure that any unsettled matters can be identified and settled. The problem of any surplus, however unlikely, is one of the matters usually raised at these meetings.

9.3.3.4 *Announcement literature.* A well-drafted announcement leaflet should be sent to each individual transferring member and proper notice given of any meetings to discuss the merger proposals. Benefit comparison, even when an uplifted scale is being offered, should be set out in detail. And it must always be accepted that there will be dissentient members who either cannot or do not wish to understand that the benefits offered are not to their disadvantage.

9.3.3.5 *Position of dissentients.* The normal provision for dissentients is to state simply that they will be treated as non-contracted-out employees and given paid-up annuities for their accrued benefits on the scale of entitlement for early leavers in their old scheme.

9.3.3.6 *Disposal of actuarial surplus.* The disposal of any actuarial surplus following the purchase of the employees' promised benefits in the new merged scheme must also be carefully explained. If the new benefits for transferring current contributors already give full equated years credit for past pensionable service, it would certainly cause considerable personnel problems if these were to be improved. The only practicable solution in such circumstances is to improve existing pensions in payment (of the old scheme) and any deferred or reversionary pensions, in that order, unless there is sufficient surplus, say, to provide a continuing rate of escalation rather than a one-off improvement.

9.3.3.7 *Meetings of members.* In some older schemes, as has been mentioned previously, provision is made for any fundamental changes in the status of the pension scheme or its trustee arrangements to be subject to the votes of the members, normally only the current contributing members. The pension scheme manager will be responsible for the careful supervision of any such meetings and the legal adviser and the actuary should also be present to ensure that the proceedings are not invalidated by any technical oversights. The task of retracing the procedure and endangering the success of the whole scheme merger should not be underestimated.

9.3.3.8 *Transfer of securities.* The final responsibility of the scheme manager will be to ensure that the securities and cash representing the underlying assets are transferred following the successful outcome of the merger meeting and for approval of the transferring members.

If the transfer of the share portfolio is to be split between several external fund managers, this will require careful forward planning prior to the actual merger date. With forethought, it is possible to avoid any large-scale disruption in the pattern of the share portfolio by encouraging the fund managers to indicate preferences. The final decision as to allocation must rest with the pension scheme manager and his trustee board.

9.3.4 *Scheme merger checklist*

The following should be covered:
(1) *Comparison of benefits between schemes.*
    Actuarial assumptions used.
    Benefit structure.

Basis of pensionable/final pensionable salary.
Integration with State scheme/duplication of benefit.
Allowance for early/late retirement.
Escalation built in/discretionary.
Contribution/funding rates.
Contracted out arrangements/benefits.
(2) *Sundry items needing investigation.*
Any recent improvements in schemes.
Non-funded discretionary pension increases.
Sickness and permanent ill-health pensions pending.
Any purchased life annuities with external insurers.
Any unpurchased past service benefits (insured scheme).
(3) *Merger sequence.*
Examination of trust deeds/amendments.
Provision in rules for members to vote on changes.
Trustee action/resolutions: scheme amendments.
Actuarial valuations/disposal of surplus.
Management/allocation of responsibility for deficit.
Any Advisory/Consultative Committees.
Documentation programme/legal and actuarial.
Literature/application forms for joining.
Consultation arrangements/unions/members' meetings.

9.4 Conclusion

(1) Company takeovers and pension scheme mergers are some of the most difficult responsibilities of a pension scheme manager.
(2) Different criteria apply to the sale of part-undertakings, not involving the eventual closure of a scheme, and to the merger of entire companies with existing pension schemes of their own.
(3) Except for preservation of statutory pension rights, transferring employees would seem to have little built-in protection, and *best practice* is for employers to recognise the importance now attached to the protection of pension rights in the case of involuntary transfers of employment.
(4) Proposed legislation in 1984 is likely to improve the protection of deferred pensions, both by revaluation and the abolition of franking, but it seems improbable that it will affect accrued benefits before the date of the actual enactments.

10 Control of fund investments

For the purposes of this chapter, a pension fund will be defined as a scheme which is approved under FA 1970, and so far as its investment activities are concerned it is exempt from income tax, corporation tax and capital gains tax.

Furthermore, its investments may be self-administered, the employer may use an external or an in-house investment fund manager or managers or it may be an insured scheme, with the investments managed by an insurance company which will also guarantee the benefits.

It is, of course, possible to have a combination of the insured and self-invested methods. The terms of reference used for this chapter have excluded certain other types of scheme which are not particularly common at the present time. An example of such a scheme would be one which is 'closed', in which investments are held only to provide pensions for a limited group of people who may no longer be contributing to the scheme.

Such closed schemes have special investment problems which are beyond the scope of this book. Suffice it to say that when such a situation arises, considerable reliance will be placed on the ownership of gilt-edged or other high quality fixed interest securities with maturity dates which match the emerging liabilities of the closed fund.

10.1 Why have investments?

It is perfectly possible, although not necessarily wise, for an employer to set up a pension scheme where the benefits are paid out of monies solely provided by the employer out of revenues. Such a scheme would, of course, be heavily dependent upon the consistency of profits of the employer and in most circumstances would not give much security to the pensioner or prospective pensioner. This type of scheme is to be found on the Continent and is generally known as a 'Book Reserve Scheme'.

Nearly all employers (and the government by virtue of the tax exemptions on investment activities which it gives) recognise that a more secure base for the payment of pensions can be achieved by setting aside monies in a trust fund and investing them in a variety of Stock Exchange and other securities. Such a trust fund will consist of the contributions of the employer, the contributions of the employee (in the case of a contributory fund), and the investment income from previously acquired investments and those assets themselves.

The management of the trust fund will be carried out by the trustees who are normally appointed by the employer (but increasingly from names put forward for appointment by an elective process carried out in conjunction with trade unions and other employee representative bodies).

While all the duties of the trustees are extremely important (and they are dealt with elsewhere in this book), among the most onerous is the investment of the trust property.

The manner in which the trustees carry out their investment responsibilities will be governed by the trust deed or other instrument under which the pension scheme is constituted. Most, if not all, modern trust deeds will have a specific investment clause which will permit the trustees to invest over a wide range which enables them to take full advantage of the various investment outlets available to them.

10.2 Investment policy

No matter whether the funds are self-administered, internally or externally managed or wholly managed by an insurance company, the trustees cannot abrogate their responsibility for the investments of the scheme. It is, therefore, important that the essentials of policy-making are fully understood.

Investment policy will be a function of the requirements of the scheme. The vast majority of present-day pension schemes are what are known as 'final-salary' or 'defined-benefit' schemes. In this type of scheme, the pension payable is linked to the salary of the pensioner before retirement (perhaps the average of the last five years, three years or, more commonly these days, the salary in the final year).

Final-salary schemes have the merit of at least making sure that the pension, when first paid, has taken account of inflationary movements in salaries up to the point of retirement. Such a link is an important factor in the type of investment policy followed.

While final-salary schemes are now the most common, the money purchase or defined-contribution schemes cannot be totally ignored (and they have come back into the limelight following the recent decline in the rate of inflation). Clearly, an investment policy designed to cater for inflation, at least to the point of retirement, will be quite different from one which does not attempt to do this.

If it is assumed that the type of pension scheme for which investment policy is being determined is of the final-salary type, then certain factors have to be taken into account in its formulation. First, the policy horizon will be a long one. A new entrant to a scheme may have a working life of 30 to 40 years and a further 15 to 20 years on pension.

Secondly, there may be certain advantages of such long time horizons: such as the ability to take a view on certain types of initially low-income investments which may have the prospects of growth and capital gain. There are also severe disadvantages in that investment targets for a final-salary-type scheme are in many ways open-ended. This is particularly the case where the employer endeavours to take account of inflation by escalating the level of pensions in payment.

It is against this background that investment policy must be determined. The mix of assets between conventional gilt-edged stocks, index-linked gilt-edged stocks, equities and properties will be a response to the open-ended nature of liabilities in a final-salary scheme.

Much has been written and will no doubt continue to be written on the theory and practice of investment management and a great deal of published work (a lot of it American) exists. However, before delving into the intricacies of these works, there are certain basic practical considerations which need to be understood. These are dealt with below.

10.3 The framework of investment policy

There are various collectors of statistics who describe how pension funds invest their funds between the various sectors available to them. These include the Central Statistical Office of HM Government, the Government Actuary's Department and the Annual Survey of the NAPF. The figures quoted in Table 1 have been taken (with permission) from the eighth annual survey of the NAPF published in 1982, which probably covers about half the employed persons in the UK, who are members of occupational pension schemes.

To understand why the assets are distributed in the way they are, it is necessary to know a little about the nature of each of the assets in terms of its risk and return characteristics. It is also necessary to understand the basic needs of the pension fund in investment terms. As already mentioned, it is a very long term institution with a need for growing returns to enable pensions to be paid which match final salaries. These will themselves be growing partly in real terms, as the individual scheme member progresses throughout his career, and partly in money terms as inflation continues. The investments in which pension fund monies are placed

Table 1. Distribution for all funded schemes taking part in the 1983 NAPF survey.

	Market values £m	All schemes %
Cash & short-term deposits	1,730.3	3
Fixed interest	11,466.6	21
Equities (including convertibles)	21,154.6	39
Property (excluding property unit trusts)	10,795.6	20
Property unit trusts	1,502.5	3
Overseas securities:		
Equities	5,009.5	10
Other	1,734.9	3
Other investments	508.4	1
	£53,90.4m	100

must also be secure because, as discussed above, perhaps the prime reason for having a funded pension scheme is the security it offers to the member. This fund must be quite separate and independent of the employer's business.

Herein lies the essential dilemma for the investment of pension fund monies. Investments which are secure such as British government securities and other fixed interest investments offer very little in the way of long-term growth. Investments which do offer growth of income and capital such as equities and property can be extremely risky when taken in isolation. Of course, risks can be lessened by buying a spread of stocks, and this is exactly what pension funds do in the equity and property markets.

Property has characteristics which are different again from those of fixed interest stocks and equities. Provided a property is let to a good commercial tenant, rentals are a very secure form of investment income. Property is relatively unmarketable so that only large schemes can hold property directly. Property unit trusts have, however, enabled the small funds to overcome this apparent disadvantage.

Index-linked gilts have been available since 1981 and combine many of the most desirable features required from an investment for pension funds. They offer the security of the conventional gilt-edged stocks and the possibility of a real return over the level of inflation. The only problem is that there are not (and are unlikely to be) enough of them to satisfy the needs of pension funds where total assets currently are in the region of £100 billion.

If risk is one major factor which must be considered when choosing the asset mix for a pension fund, the other major factor is the return which they offer. On the face of it, there would appear to be no contest between a conventional gilt yielding 10%, an equity yielding 4.5% and a property yielding between 3.5% and 7%.

To understand why pension funds are not wholly invested in conventional gilt-edged stocks it is necessary to understand the concept of total return. If the redemption yield on a gilt is 10% then that is the yield to the purchaser for the rest of the life of the stock. The initial yield of 4.5% on the equity can grow as dividends increase. It is not difficult to demonstrate mathematically that the true comparable yield on the equity is, over longish periods of time, the sum of the initial yield plus the annual percentage growth in that return.

Thus, with dividend growth of 10% per annum, the total return on an equity whose initial yield is 4.5% is 14.5%. This can be directly compared with the redemption yield of 10% on the conventional gilt-edged stock. The advent of index-linked stocks does not in any way invalidate this piece of analysis. It simply means that in comparing conventional gilts and equities to index-linked stocks, the annual rate of inflation must first be deducted from the total returns on the conventional gilt and the equity.

The investment fund manager must take into account the risk factors and the return factors outlined above in making his decision about the asset mix of the fund. That mix must reflect the apparent conflict between absolute security and the need for growth.

10.4 How pension fund investments are managed

As explained in the opening paragraphs of this chapter, the trustees cannot abrogate their responsibilities for the investment of their pension fund. This does not mean, of course, that they cannot take expert advice. Indeed, in every case they should do so.

If the trustees are engaged in setting up a new fund, they have a number of choices as to how the investment will be managed.

The first, and on the face of it, the simplest way is to pass the whole problem to an insurance company. For very small and small funds up to about £5 million, this is probably the preferred method. However, it must be remembered that insurance companies are not philanthropic organisations and the charges for such a service can be considerable.

Where the fund is larger and the trustees wish to take a more direct interest in the investment role, they may choose an external manager or managers to look after the fund. The process of choice of an external fund manager is dealt with more fully in Chapter 2. The trustees will certainly need expert advice for this process.

10.5 Internal or external management?

For the fund with assets up to about £100 million, the choice between internal and external management is not a difficult one. A merchant bank will charge about 0.1% annually on the value of the assets under management. The charge for a £100 million fund would, therefore, be £100,000 and it is obvious that it would not be possible to employ an in-house manager for this sum of money after allowing for the usual office overheads. Beyond the £100 million mark, the decision to employ an in-house manager will become easier as the size of the fund increases, but much will depend upon the management philosophy of the company concerned.

10.6 External management

As only about 12 per cent of pension funds had assets over £100 million in 1983 (NAPF survey), the majority of management will be faced with the problem of selecting an external manager.

What should be looked for in the selection process and what help should be sought in carrying it out is outlined in Chapter 2.

What sort of questions should the potential client be asking? The following is a checklist, which although by no means exhaustive, will go a long way to achieving the correct result.

10.6.1 *External manager checklist*

(1) *The investment fund manager*

The following questions should be asked:
  (a) What is the nature of the organisation – bank, merchant bank, broker, independent adviser?
  (b) How long has it been managing pension fund investments?
  (c) How many pension funds does it manage and what is the total of assets under management?

(2) *Investment philosophy*

The questions to be asked are as follows:
  (a) What is the manager's attitude to the various sectors (gilts, equities, property, overseas markets)?
  (b) Is this in accord with the client's basic approach to the various sectors?
  (c) Is the manager equity or fixed interest orientated?

(3) *What is the manager's decision-making structure?*
  (a) How does he arrive at overall investment policy?
  (b) How does he arrive at the division between UK and overseas assets?
  (c) How does he go about sector analysis and stock selection?
  (d) How does he do research – does he separate research from fund management or is it an integral part of the fund manager's task?

(4) *Management structure*
  (a) How many managers does the firm employ? What is their background and experience?
  (b) Who will actively look after the fund? What is his/her background, experience and qualifications?

(5) *Administration*
  (a) Does the manager offer banking services?
  (b) What kind of reports does he provide and how frequent are they? Do the reports include a valuation of the fund? How are these reports presented? Will the manager be present at the trustees' meetings?
  (c) In addition to purchases and sales, will the manager look after registration – custody collection of dividends and interest? Will he deal with rights and scrip issues? Will he reclaim tax on dividends?
(6) *Fees*
  (a) What exactly does the manager charge? Is there a minimum charge?
  (b) Does he share commission on Stock Exchange transactions or does he pass it on to the fund?
(7) *Investment performance record*
  This subject is dealt with in greater detail in Chapter 11, but the basic questions to be asked are as follows:
  (a) Who measures the performance and
  (b) How consistent is the record over a period of years? (Beware of brilliant single-year performance figures.)

Finally, when checklists have been completed, the client must feel comfortable with the firm and the individual manager who is going to look after the fund. He must be prepared to give the manager a chance to perform – a run of at least three to five years must be a minimum. The form of the agreement is discussed in Chapter 2 and an example is shown as Appendix 1.

10.7 Internal management

There will come a point, whether it be when the share portfolio reaches a market value of £200 million or £300 million of assets, when the trustees must consider the possibility of employing an internal investment manager. They should first consider the disadvantages. It will be expensive; a manager will need support, if only secretarial and administration; he will need to take holidays and he will occasionally go sick. He will need very careful selection; once appointed, he may be very expensive to dismiss and he may do untold damage before he can be dismissed.

In addition, the trustees will have to be prepared to be much more involved with the investment process. They will need to form an investment committee which will need to meet at least quarterly and probably monthly. How much discretion will the trustees be prepared to give the internal manager? If he is given too much, he may cause irreparable damage; if he is given too little, he may be too inhibited to act effectively.

All this may sound very daunting, but nevertheless many companies do take the plunge and appoint an internal investment manager. Saving costs cannot be the prime consideration for doing this, but the opportunity to have a manager who has only one client can be very rewarding.

11 Investment performance

Accurate measurement of the overall performance of a pension fund's investments is essential in order to help the trustees to discharge their most important responsibility – namely, the safeguarding of the fund.

The existence of an independent performance-measuring service, providing comparative information about the investments on a regular and consistent basis, will enable the trustees to have a better understanding of the long term problems of pension fund management. With the help of quarterly reports and a consolidated annual performance report, the trustees will be able to recognise and accept short-term variations in the performance of individual holdings and the main share sectors. Performance trends shown up in the annual reports will also help the trustees to assess any recommendations from the fund managers for changes in the relative balance between main sectors of the investment portfolio to secure improvement in the overall return on the fund.

Details of the relative performance of the individual fund managers and the performance of the fund as a whole by comparison with other similar funds will form an integral part of the service provided by any major performance consultant.

11.1 Why measure investment performance?

A number of reasons can be advanced for trustees spending money on an assessment of their pension fund's investment performance. The reasons are as follows:

11.1.1 *To monitor the progress of investments*

The trustees of many pension schemes invest in a range of investments, either directly, or indirectly through a managed fund, a unit trust or a deposit administration contract, where the future value of those investments cannot be determined at the outset.

The benefits of the pension fund will usually be denominated either in terms of a fraction of the member's salary close to retirement or as a fixed monetary sum, and the trustees will need to chart the progress of their investments to ensure that they will be able to pay the benefits as they fall due.

Investment in certain types of asset will increase the likelihood of a greater overall return for the fund, but this will probably be accompanied by a higher chance of failing to secure the required level of return. Trustees will, therefore, need to monitor the overall spread of investments, the return from each class of investment, and their associated levels of risk.

11.1.2 *To ascertain the relative performance*

Most trustees employ expert investment fund managers, either directly or indirectly (if they invest in a managed fund, unit trust or deposit administration contract), and the trustees need to ascertain whether the manager is doing a good, bad or indifferent job when compared with other managers of funds in a similar position.

11.1.3 *To analyse past performance and allocate future resources*

The overall return on a pension fund will depend upon the following:
(1) The proportion held in each of the various asset categories (the strategy).
(2) The returns on the actual assets held within each asset category (the choice of stocks).

If the contribution to the overall return is split between these two factors, the trustees can see the relative importance of each in the past, and this will hopefully enable resources to be concentrated on the most important areas in the future and facilitate corrective action where the performance was relatively poor. All too often, trustee meetings are dominated by a discussion of the relative merits of individual shares, and in many such cases it can be shown that the performance of the United Kingdom portfolio is closely in line with the market averages and has little effect on the overall result. It may be better to allocate more of the time at trustee meetings to a discussion of the strategy decision which has tended to be the main determinant of performance, and to let the manager use his expertise in selecting individual shares.

11.1.4 *To identify managers with above-average track records*

Performance measurement also enables trustees to identify investment managers with a good track record for the past and to be aware of managers' characteristics, strengths and weaknesses before an appointment is made. When performance figures are requested, nearly every prospective manager seems to be able to produce some statistics indicating an above-average past performance, and the use of a consistent and objective basis for performance analysis provides a rational basis for assessing each manager's claims.

11.2 Over what period should performance be measured?

A pension fund has long-term liabilities and hence it is a continuing long-term exercise to determine whether the investments are achieving a satisfactory performance to enable the benefits to be paid when they fall due. The investment strategy followed may be for the long term, but in recent years external managers have tended to invest using a fairly short-term horizon. This trend may be because of the view that the long term is a succession of short terms, the investment outlook is clouded with uncertainty, or because some performance measurement services have unfortunately focused attention on short-term results.

Emphasis on short-term figures may discourage managers from taking remedial action which may be necessary for good long-term performance, because they do not wish the expenses or size of any change to reduce their short-term performance figures. If managers receive too much criticism on short-term results, they may veer towards a 'near average' policy. If the asset distribution is moved close to that of the average fund, and the shares within each sector invested fairly conventionally in line with the market averages, the overall results in each period are likely to be close to average. This means that if the results are a little above average the trustees and the manager will be happy, but if they are a little below average, they will not be far enough below average to get the manager sacked!

For most funds the short-term figures are not likely to be a good guide to the longer-term results and, unless the manager has disastrous results, trustees should assess the ability of their investment manager over at least one stock market cycle. Stock market cycles are of varying lengths, but such an assessment shows how the manager copes in conditions of rising and falling security prices. This usually means waiting at least five years before reaching a firm conclusion about the manager's ability. A longer period may be necessary where an unconventional investment philosophy is used but due to the higher levels of risk often involved in these cases, trustees cannot let an adverse situation continue indefinitely.

Short-term figures for single quarters or single years may be useful to see trends established or to assess short-term market timing, but trustees should think carefully before dismissing a manager with good long-term (five years or more) performance and with poor shorter-term results, unless they are convinced that the short-term position is unlikely to reverse. It is not as easy as many suggest to select managers who are likely to achieve above average returns in the future, and it is all too easy to go out of the frying-pan and into the fire when the manager is changed!

11.3 Common methods of measurement

There are many methods which can be used to measure the investment return on a fund, and the appropriate method depends on the question that the calculations are designed to answer. For example, is the purpose to calculate the rate of return which has been earned on the pension fund assets over a particular period, or is it to compare the performance of several different investment managers? Whatever the question, it is vital to have this clearly in mind when looking at the results.

The methods generally in use assume that funds are invested to obtain the highest overall rate of return from income and capital combined, and take into account both income received and changes in market value. Since funds generally have much more investment income and contributions than benefit outgo, it is assumed that there is no need to sell investments to pay benefits, and no requirement for a specified level of current income.

Market prices midway between the buying and selling prices (mid-market prices) are generally used as the measure of the value of an asset at each point in time in performance assessment even though funds could not necessarily sell their holdings at a price equal to this value. The price used is the same for all funds and enables the success of various alternative strategies to be determined, even though market prices are not necessarily too relevant for a fund that has no need to sell assets to pay benefits. The use of market values also provides a rate at which income can be exchanged into capital and vice versa.

11.3.1 *The money-weighted rate of return*

If calculations are intended to measure the rate of return which has been earned on the assets of the fund, then the money-weighted rate of return may be the appropriate measure. The money-weighted rate of return is that used in discounted cashflow calculations.

For algebra enthusiasts, this can be specified as follows:

If the initial market value of the portfolio is M_1, the final market value at time n is M_2 and C_j is the amount of the contribution made at time t_j before the end of the period, then the annual money-weighted rate of return i may be found from

$$M_1(1 + i)^n +_j\Sigma \times C_j(1 + i)t_j = M_2.$$

The rate of return i will be influenced by the timing and magnitude of the cashflows, as can be seen from the following simplified and rather extreme example. Let us suppose that there are two funds, A and B. The market value of both funds falls from 100 to 50 at the middle of the year and then Fund B receives a cash injection of 100. Fund A now has assets of 50 and Fund B, assets of 150. During the second half of the year, both funds double the value of their assets, so at the year end Fund A has assets of 100 and Fund B, assets of 300. This can be shown in the following way:

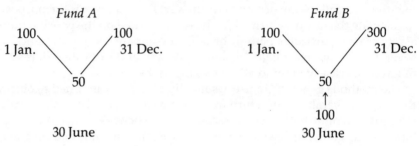

The money-weighted rate of return for Fund A is

$$100 (1 + i) = 100$$
$$i = 0\%$$

and for B it is

$$100 (1 + i) + 100 (1 + i)^{\frac{1}{2}} = 300$$
$$i = 69.7\%.$$

However, the manager of Fund A has seen the value of his assets under management halve in the first half of the year and double in the second half. So has the investment manager of Fund B. So, although both managers achieve similar performances on the assets under management, the money-weighted rates of return differ substantially, because Fund B was fortunate to receive some new money at the bottom of the market.

The incidence and magnitude of new money flows are outside the control of fund managers and so any method which attempts to compare the performances of different managers should eliminate the effect of new money flows.

11.3.2 *The time-weighted rate of return*

The time-weighted rate of return method seeks to eliminate the distorting effect of new money flows by calculating the market value of the assets each time there is a cash flow and taking the product of the ratios of successive valuations. In other words, it examines the performance of a representative slice of the fund.

Taking the above example, the calculations of the time-weighted rate of return would be as follows:

Fund A

$$(1 + i) = \frac{50}{100} \times \frac{100}{50}$$

$$i = 0\%$$

Fund B

$$(1 + i) = \frac{50}{100} \times \frac{300}{150}$$

$$i = 0\%$$

The rates of return in this example are similar using this method but there is an additional problem in that the use of this method requires a valuation of the fund each time there is a cash flow. This is not a practical proposition for the vast majority of funds, so that some approximation is needed which will produce a close and hopefully unbiased estimate of the true time-weighted rate of return. The method usually used is the 'linked internal rate of return'. Periods of one-quarter of a year are used and the money-weighted rate of return is calculated for each quarter. The rates are then linked together so that if, for example, the calculated rates for four quarters were 1%, 2%, 3% and 4%, the linked internal rate of return for the year would be as follows:

$$1.01 \times 1.02 \times 1.03 \times 1.04 = 1.104, \text{ i.e. } 10.4\%$$

Since only one quarter is considered at a time, the importance of the new money relative to the money already in the fund is considerably reduced, but the procedure does not entirely eliminate the effect of new money flows. If periods shorter than one quarter are selected, then a closer approximation to the true time-weighted rate of return would be achieved. The shorter the time period, the more extensive the data and the number of calculations required; hence a reasonable balance must be obtained between increased administration and increased accuracy.

11.3.3 *The unit price method*

The value of a holding in a unit trust or in an insurance-company-managed fund is obtained by dividing the value of the securities held by the unit trust or the managed fund by the number of units in issue to obtain the unit price. The unit price can form the basis of a performance measurement, but it may not answer the question of how well the securities in the unit trust or managed fund have performed. This is because the manager usually has some latitude for changing the basis on which the unit price is calculated relative to the value of the underlying securities, according to whether buyers or sellers of units predominate.

Furthermore, the expenses of participation in some managed funds may be dealt with before money is passed to the managed fund, whereas in others the expenses are taken from the fund. This latter problem may mean that two managed funds with identical securities and identical security performance would show different unit price changes, just because one of the funds asks participants to pay its charges before investing and the other receives its remuneration from the managed fund itself.

11.3.4 *Complications from property investments*

Market prices for Stock Exchange securities can easily be obtained on an objective and consistent basis, but property values are only available when valuations are carried out and even then contain a subjective element depending on the whim of the valuer. Property cannot be instantly purchased or sold in the same way as Stock Exchange assets, and this, coupled with the variety of valuation frequencies and valuation methods in use, suggests that property performance should be measured over lengthy periods (e.g. over five years or longer). Even then the margins of error in property return calculations are generally much higher than for Stock Exchange assets, and it is unlikely that it will be possible to measure the relative abilities of a property manager.

Despite these very real difficulties and the limitations of the returns, it is still all too easy to point to league tables of returns including property which appear to ignore these difficulties. Returns on property assets should, therefore, be treated with great caution, and if conclusions are made it is worth making sure that the conclusions can be substantiated from the system of measurement in use.

11.4 What comparisons can be made with the returns?

11.4.1 *Comparison with other funds*

Once returns have been calculated, the next stage is to make some comparison between the returns and some yardstick. The choice of yardstick will depend to a great extent on the purpose of the calculations. When making comparisons, it is necessary to compare like with like. Some of the problems associated with comparisons of returns on this basis were illustrated above and only limited comparisons are possible on a money-weighted basis.

In general, most of the questions asked relate to the relative abilities of fund managers and hence it is normally appropriate to use the time-weighted rate or unit price methods.

The natural method of comparison is to compare the returns of a pension fund with those of other funds with similar characteristics. The characteristics could be those of size, level of cash flow, nature of the liabilities, constraints on the investment manager and the level of risk which is acceptable to the trustees. If pension funds were divided according to just these criteria, then it would only be possible to compare the returns for a fund with those of a few other funds. A large sample size would be much more desirable if it was still possible to maintain a like-with-like comparison.

In the United Kingdom most self-administered pension funds have final-salary-type liabilities and, as mentioned above, are in the position of not having to realise assets for the foreseeable future. With the levels of inflation experienced in recent years, and the uncertain investment conditions which have prevailed, funds have generally made little or no allowance for the maturity of their liabilities when framing investment policy.

In addition, very few investment managers are hampered by investment constraints which cannot easily be changed by reference to the trustees, and most constraints are really better described as investment guidelines until the next trustees' meeting. Usually, any actual constraints which are set down are to prevent transactions in the parent company's securities or possibly those of competitors, and this type of constraint is likely to have only a very marginal effect on investment performance.

These considerations make it possible to substantially enlarge the sample which can be used. The sample size could be further increased if it was found that the returns were independent of the size of the fund and the level of cash flow. The evidence available does not indicate a strong link between size and return, or, apart from short periods, between the cash flow of a fund and returns. The returns of final-salary pension plans can, therefore, be compared together, and the advantages of using a larger sample size probably outweigh the disadvantages of combining funds with insignificant differences in characteristics.

11.4.2 Notional funds

A further yardstick for making comparisons is the notional fund. This is a fund which invested at some date in various sectors in certain specified proportions and each sector performs in line with a stated index. For example, a fund which invested 60% in equities and 40% in fixed interest assets may be used where a 60:40 ratio is considered to be a reasonable long-term asset mix (or is the investment manager's current guideline) and the aim of the investment manager is supposedly to outperform this notional fund.

Notional fund comparisons were common in the 1960s and early 1970s before inter-fund comparison services were widely available.

Notional funds have a number of difficulties which are as follows:

(1) A fund which starts at 60:40 will alter from this ratio since equities and gilts are unlikely to move in tandem. If the fund is rebalanced to 60:40 periodically, this will involve 'selling' the best performing asset and 'buying' the worst. This is a procedure which cannot be a practical proposition for the fund manager and hence the comparison is somewhat artificial.

(2) The fundamental element in the overall performance is usually the sector split (i.e. the 60:40 ratio in this example). The method assumes that 60:40 ratio is correct and does not focus attention on whether it

really is, or whether other alternatives would have been more
profitable.

(3) There are several varieties of notional fund, and each can produce
useful results when it is clearly understood what it is setting out to
measure; however, notional funds can easily result in incorrect
conclusions in the hands of unskilled users.

11.5 Investment performance analysts

There are many firms which offer to measure the performance of pension
funds. Some trustees use the same firm as that providing their normal
actuarial advice, but performance measurement is a specialised area, and
it may be more logical to seek out the best investment performance
service.

The measurement service should offer very readable reports rather
than just a mountain of statistics and, perhaps of greater importance, a
team of investment specialists who can discuss the reports with the
trustees. Participation in a service is likely to be much more useful if the
trustees can make time to go through a report and to ensure that they
appreciate the conclusions which it is appropriate to make from it.

The comparisons with the results of other funds (or other unit trusts,
deposit administration contracts or managed funds) should cover as
many funds as possible, and it is important that the sample is not biased
by the inclusion of many funds by a single institution. Even large samples
can contain a high level of bias and not give trustees a balanced view.

Trustees should try to ensure that the sample provides a wide range of
funds and that each investment manager is represented in the service
broadly in line with his general share of the pension fund investment
management market. Services which have only been running for a short
time may not be able to provide the spread which is desirable, and this is
more likely to be found in the long-established services.

11.6 The investment manager's reaction to the results of performance measurement

Investment managers are now accustomed to participating in investment
performance services, and few managers are likely to dispute the main
methods in use. Some managers may have been worried that performance measurement would just be a destructive weapon for the trustees to
make their life difficult, but many now see it as a very helpful and
constructive aid in their relationship with trustees. The manager is now
less likely to be sacked if the trustees think that the performance is
inadequate when it isn't!

If the investment manager can be present when the investment performance analyst discusses his report with the trustees, this should result
in a more productive use of the report and tends to avoid any doubts

which the investment manager may have on the use of investment performance statistics. Part of this investment measurement process will be an analysis of the past and the reasons for this past performance, but any implications from the past for future investment policy need to be discussed with the investment manager and cannot really be considered just by the trustees and the investment performance analyst.

Investment managers are also able to use performance figures to show the practical effect of various courses of action and the trustees can then see the effect on return of different levels of risk.

If there are several investment managers, the process of analysis and discussion of the results is more complex. Most trustees keep the exact performance of the other managers a secret, but use the figures in general terms to keep each manager continually on his toes. In this way, any complacency from a good performance can be avoided. Other funds give full disclosure of other managers' returns, and hope that managers will be shamed into improvement. Whatever method is used, it is important for managers to concentrate on producing sound long-term performance for the trustees rather than a good short-term return.

11.7 Conclusion

Performance measurement is a vital component of the information needed by trustees to ensure the effective investment of their assets. It does cost money to measure performance (although some stockbrokers may sponsor services on behalf of their clients so that the cost is paid by the client in terms of Stock Exchange commission), but trustees should find that this money is well spent.

12 Relationship of trustees and employer company

The opinion is often expressed that it is impossible for the same person to exercise impartial judgement as a trustee while at the same time occupying a substantive position in the management of the employer company, possibly as a director. The conflict of interest may appear insuperable. Yet this is not the case in practice and an experienced executive finds little difficulty in 'wearing two hats' and having two separate responsibilities. A similar situation exists in the case of the shop steward or union activist who is made a member trustee. Like the management-nominated trustee, he would indeed be in breach of his trustee responsibilities if he did not act impartially on behalf of both union and non-union members. In practice, he carries out the responsibilities of his two jobs to the best of his ability.

The same argument, therefore, applies equally to management-nominated trustees and to member trustees. Without this ability, it would indeed be difficult for occupational pension schemes to function as successfully as they have in the rapidly changing circumstances of the last decade, with all the many statutory developments in the pensions field and the very considerable extension of membership participation, particularly at trustee board level.

12.1 Principles governing the relationship between trustees and company

Some of the more important principles governing the relationship between the trustee board and the company are as follows:

(1) The powers and responsibilities of the trustees are governed entirely by the terms of the trust deed and the rules. The trustees are

appointed to protect the interests of the beneficiaries, and to safe-guard the funds entrusted to their care by both company and employee but which can only be used for the benefit of members of the scheme and their dependants.

(2) The trustees have no absolute power to change any of the rules without the direction or concurrence of the employer company. But even then, the employer company cannot unilaterally reduce benefits without the consent of the members and the trustees have the right and duty to point this out.

(3) By reason of the restrictions imposed in the trust deed and rules, it must be the company to whom the members must look to improve the scheme or amend the rules and not the trustees.

(4) Under the provisions of the SSPA 1975 and subsequent statutory amendments, the OPB has in certain circumstances an overriding power to impose mandatory alterations to the trust deed of an exempt approved pension scheme. But in those cases, it will still be the company which will have to authorise the trustees to make the necessary formal amendments to the rules.

12.2 A pension scheme and its financial relationship with the parent company

Reference to the trust deed governing the pension scheme will show the clear distinction which lies between the employer – generally referred to as the principal company – and the trustees who are given a firm responsibility for the collection of the fund income and the management of the capital financial resources, which together constitute the pension fund.

12.2.1 *Collection of normal annual contributions*

Once the pension scheme has been established and has received the necessary statutory approval required by FA 1970, the principal employer becomes obligated by the trust deed to hand over the contributions/ premium monies necessary to provide the benefits promised to the members. For a contributory scheme that would also include the collec-tion of the members' share of the contribution income.

Particularly in insured schemes, the trust deed will probably provide that the employer finds the balance of the annual cost of running the scheme on the contributions (normal annual) deemed necessary by the actuaries. Even in final-salary schemes, this provision is not uncommon, but there is generally a fall-back clause in the trust deed allowing the employer to terminate this obligation on giving the requisite period of notice.

It is, thus, very important that this fixed overhead should be expressed as a certain cost in order to establish the effect on current trading costs.

12.2.2 *Special contributions*

Another form of annual cost can be in the provision of special contributions or, more properly, a phased spread of the capital cost of funding any benefits over and above those governed by the normal contributions.

For example, at a time of mergers, a new section of membership may join the company pension scheme, but with an insufficient amount of transferred assets from their former scheme to cover the cost of providing past service benefits promised under the provisions of the former scheme.

If there is a vending agreement (see Chapter 9), it would generally cover this aspect by providing that the purchaser (or the new participating company) should meet the additional funding costs, e.g. by an actuarially determined amount payable in a single sum or over such a period as is permitted by the Revenue. An alternative method would be for the purchase price payable to the vendor to be abated, if the responsibility for securing the necessary funding rested with the vendor.

12.3 Areas of possible conflict of interest

The most common areas where conflict can arise in the relationship between the trustee board and the principal company are as follows:

12.3.1 *Personal status of trustees*

There is the conflict between the responsibility of the trustee to the pension scheme and his position as an employee member of the pension scheme. The methods of ensuring that new trustees are helped to become conversant with their new responsibilities are set out in Chapter 7.

12.3.2 *Trust deed matters*

While the financial limits of the trustees' discretionary powers, e.g. for augmentation of pensions, are generally set out clearly in the trust deed, the trustees may also have to play a positive role when difficulties arise in connection with the following parts of the trust deed:

12.3.2.1 *The alteration clause.* This will usually read: 'The trustees may with the consent of the principal company, from time to time amend the scheme . . . but no such alteration shall be made which will have the effect of . . .'. In practice, this means that the onus is on the principal company to initiate any amendments and for the trustees to ensure that they come within the powers set out in the rules.

Certain matters such as preservation of accrued benefits laid down by statute cannot be altered, but there are exceptional circumstances where the employer company may have to negotiate a reduction of benefits and/ or an increase in contribution rates, and the trust deed should set out the procedure for such negotiation or consultation. A reduction could only apply to future benefits; full financial provision should already have been made for accrued benefits.

12.3.2.2 *Any overriding guarantee of solvency of the fund.* This guarantee by the principal company, sometimes expressed as a guaranteed rate of return on the invested capital, is seldom found in modern trust deeds because of the open-ended nature of the liability in inflationary times. It could merely serve to make the employer company insolvent and bring the pension scheme itself to an unnecessary conclusion.

Cases have occurred in recent years where an employer has actually negotiated reduction of benefits and contributions in order to enable the company to keep trading.

It is in these circumstances that the skill and experience of the management trustee is brought fully into play.

12.3.2.3 *Power of termination.* This clause will normally provide 'that the company may, on giving, say, six months' notice to the trustees of its intention so to do, terminate the payment of contributions', thus effectively bringing the scheme to a close.

In such circumstances, the 'priorities rules clause' will come into effect, which sets out the priority of accrued benefits including those benefits which have to be preserved by law such as the GMP.

The power of termination is thus a fall-back if the trustees were to invoke an obligation by the company, such as to escalate pensions at an exceptionally high rate, or to meet a funding deficiency which it could not afford to pay.

12.3.3 *Adjustment of contribution levels*

The improvement of benefits and any consequential increase in cost can cause severe financial problems for the principal company unless the members are also prepared to adjust their own rate of contribution. It can, of course, happen that successive actuarial valuations have thrown up a consistent rate of surplus, which may justify an increase in benefits but should not be used to reduce existing contribution rates.

These comments do not apply to the older type of insured contract where the employer's rate of contribution is expressed as a balancing item rather than as a fixed percentage of pensionable salaries.

12.3.4 *Industrial relations*

The preliminary consultation with employees and their union representatives prior to the setting-up of a new pension scheme, or any substantial alteration of the existing benefit/contribution structure, calls for a high degree of industrial relations expertise if the process is to move smoothly within the time limits imposed. The emphasis should be on consultation, rather than negotiation.

Subsequently, the selection of member trustee representatives should proceed on the same consultative lines. Selection or election, whichever path is chosen, should appear to be manifestly a democratic process to ensure that the trustee board operates smoothly and without dispute.

If scheme members have complaints about the benefits as set out in the rules and wish to have improvements, their complaints should be directed to the company, not the trustees, preferably through the medium of a Pension Advisory Committee.

To ensure that industrial relations proceed upon the proper lines, many companies have set up a parallel organisation of Pension Advisory/ Consultative Committees specifically to avoid conflict at the trustee level (see Chapter 7).

It is usual, but not always the case, that the Advisory Committee consists solely of members of the pension scheme. They tend to be union-motivated but not always by shop stewards. It is surprising how often the pensions adviser/expert comes from the shop floor and he has an invaluable treasury of practical pensions knowledge. By no means should he be discouraged.

12.4 Special areas of company responsibility in pension scheme matters

There are certain special areas of company responsibility which are essential for the proper discharge of their undertakings as set out in the trust deed. These are given below.

12.4.1 *The composition of the trustee board*

Leaving aside those industries chiefly represented by statutory corporations in the public sector where both union representation (the closed shop) and non-member trustees are to be found, the best of present-day practice in the private sector calls for specific representation by the members on the trustee board (generally a corporate trustee company with the directors having powers analogous to those of the individual trustee).

Since the company finds the balance of the cost of funding or even the entire cost (dependent upon your views as to whether or not pensions are merely deferred pay), the company will normally require equal representation on the trustee board.

Having progressed this far, the next problem is to decide on how the chairman is to be found. This is generally a company nomination.

12.4.2 *The chairman of the trustees*

This is certainly the most important post on the trustee board and great care should be taken with regard to this appointment, in the following areas:

12.4.2.1 *In the preliminary documentation.* Provision should be made to ensure that the necessary powers are given to the company in the trust deed and/or the articles of association of the corporate trustee to settle the manner and duration of the chairman's appointment.

Where there is a corporate trustee, and this is the *preferred practice*, particularly where investment powers are concerned, the principal company in its capacity as the controlling shareholder should be given clear authority to appoint the chairman.

12.4.2.2 *In the manner of the appointment.* The appointment should be in strict accordance with the manner laid down in the preliminary documentation. Where member trustees are being appointed and a trustee board set up for the first time, even if the company has reserved the power of appointment, the member trustees should have prior knowledge of the company's intention and the details of the person to be appointed. This can be done through the Pension Advisory Committees, if these exist.

The alternative method, again to be included in the documentation, would be for the trustee board to be given power to appoint the chairman, possibly alternating the choice for each term of office between a member trustee and a management trustee. In more mature schemes this method may safely be adopted, but it is not ideal in the initial stage where the quality of the individual trustees has yet to be shown in practice while they are still gaining experience.

12.4.2.3 *In the personality of the chairman.* This is an equally important aspect since the chairman must have the confidence of both the management and more particularly of the member trustees.

He also requires the confidence of the company who may well require him, under the powers given in the trust deed, to enforce financial and personnel restrictions where very easily a conflict of interest could arise.

Above all, the chairman must not appear to be 'wearing two hats'. It is probably easier to anticipate this area of possible conflict by choosing a senior executive from outside the financial or personnel departments of the parent company. He should still carry sufficient authority to have the right of access direct to the chairman of the main board even though he may not have director status in his own right.

It is a matter of debate whether the above criteria can best be met by an appointment from within the company or from an entirely independent source not directly connected with the parent company. The *best practice* is still to find a suitable nomination from within the company and in that way to ensure that the company carries some measure of indirect responsibility for the subsequent actions of the chairman of the trustee board.

12.4.3 *To establish a corporate trustee company*

During the last decade it has become an increasingly common practice, particularly for self-administered schemes, to make provision in the trust deed for a corporate trustee company to be appointed.

The directors of the corporate trustee company are, to all intents and purposes, holding a position analogous to that of individual trustees and they are expected to exercise the rights and responsibilities which would apply under the terms of the trust deed and basic trust law.

It is true that as directors they are also governed by the provisions of the Companies Acts, but this somewhat anomalous position is presently under review by a government interdepartmental committee which is examining the whole field of pension trustee law.

The advantages of using a corporate trustee are threefold:

(1) It affords continuity, particularly for the control of investments and the execution of formal documents.
(2) For VAT purposes, the Customs & Excise allow the registration of the corporate trustee of a recognised pension scheme to be joined with that of the parent company, i.e. by grouping. In this way it was possible, in most circumstances, to reduce the incidence of VAT to minimal proportions for pension fund transactions but changes in February 1984 have made this more difficult.
(3) While the existence of a corporate trustee facilitates the documentation of property transactions, there is still the overriding requirement of the Trustee Act 1925 which allows a purchaser to require the receipt of two trustees for a purchase of an interest in property. In practice, this is seldom enforced by purchasers dealing with a pension fund, but as a safeguard some schemes have executed a second trust deed with another corporate trustee, e.g. Pension Scheme Trust Company No. 2 Limited.

12.4.4 *The responsibility for determining contribution levels*

This matter is not always given the attention which its importance demands. The financial cost to the company – and for that matter to the employee – has to be reconciled with the requirements to provide the benefits set out in the trust deed rules. If, at a periodic valuation, the funding level prescribed by the consulting actuaries is shown to be insufficient to maintain the benefits or if the members through their Advisory Committees have been pressing for an improvement of benefits, it may be necessary for contributions to be increased.

If the valuation has shown a surplus which could arise either because the previous funding (i.e. contribution level) had been too high or the investment returns had been underestimated, it is understandable that the scheme members may still expect benefit improvements.

In accordance with the rules, the responsibility would fall on the employer company to make the decision to adjust the contribution rate. The only normal proviso is that any existing accrued benefits cannot be taken away from members without their consent. Nor, since contracting out, can the basic GMP be touched without endangering OPB approval of the contracting-out certificate.

If contribution rates are to be varied, the sequence as explained above is first, for the two-way consultation to be conducted by the company with members through their Advisory Committees, otherwise industrial relations can be seriously affected. Any variation must be achieved by consensus – even the distribution of an apparent valuation surplus.

Normally, *best practice* is never to reduce contribution levels but to improve benefits cautiously after, say, two successive actuarial valuations have shown a continuous trend upwards.

12.4.5 *Responsibility for industrial relations in pension matters through Pension Advisory Committees*

Reference has been made above to the modern practice of establishing Pension Advisory Committees to enable pension matters to be discussed during the ordinary course of industrial relations and so avoid unnecessary misunderstandings of the status and powers of the trustee board by ordinary employees.

Best practice is for these Advisory Committees to be composed equally of management and employee representatives, and not necessarily, but preferably, of pension scheme members. The company should always nominate the chairman, as a Pension Advisory Committee is primarily a personnel function.

The employee representation should be by the most democratic means available, i.e. election, and be drawn from every section of the company with scheme members, even if that entails some amount of staff dislocation at times of meetings. In a large group, the Pension Advisory Committees could be arranged on a pyramid-style structure with a senior representative of management to chair the main central committee which would have representatives from the regional divisional committees.

Experience has shown that, provided management show an initial enthusiasm and endeavour to make the Advisory Committees work, little industrial trouble concerning pension matters ensues. Indeed, after the course of time, the main difficulty is to secure sufficient business for the agenda, and it should be the responsibility of the pensions manager to ensure that content matter of a continuing interest should be provided for the Advisory Committee meetings.

12.4.6 *Accounting responsibilities: provision for pension costs in company accounts*

There are two areas where the costs of operating a company pension scheme have a direct effect on the company:

12.4.6.1 *In the financial accounts.*

Pension costs are generally regarded as salary costs except when there are single annual premium payments for some of the older type of insured money purchase schemes.

Best practice is to bring normal contributions both for company and employee into the payroll computer program by means of a regular fixed monthly charge. For a self-administered scheme, this has the following advantages:

(1) It spreads the burden of pension cost equally through the financial year.
(2) It provides a regular cash flow for the investment department.
(3) It enables cost centres to reconcile the charge through their wages analysis records.

Wherever possible, the pension scheme year and the company financial year should coincide. At the start of each scheme year, the membership and pensionable salaries should be reconciled with personnel records. Subsequently during the course of the scheme year, adjustments for withdrawals and movements should be built in currently, ideally by computer interface programs. Such programs provide an easier and far more accurate system than the older practices of paying over to the pension scheme the balance shown in the wages analysis columns. The normal interbranch and withdrawals movements, together with holiday and sickness absences, make the task of manual reconciliation practically impossible.

Special contributions, e.g. to meet an actuarial funding deficiency or for improving past service benefits, are normally treated as a capital payment by the company, unless the SFO allow it to be written off, either wholly or partly, as an expense in the current financial year. The pension scheme accounts should always show special contributions separately.

12.4.6.2 *In the published company accounts.*

It has been a long-standing requirement under the Companies Acts for details of pension costs for directors to be shown in the published accounts. As yet no similar requirements exist for the employees' pension scheme costs to be shown likewise.

But following the issue of ED32 by the Accounting Standards Committee, it appears highly likely and indeed inevitable that company accounts of the future will have to pay far more regard to the disclosure of both current pension contribution costs and any provisions for contingent pension funding costs. Such costs will normally arise from special contributions spread over a number of years to meet scheme benefit improvement or actuarial funding deficiencies revealed in a valuation.

These sums can be very substantial although the SFO endeavour to exercise control over the use of special contributions by limiting their allowance as a taxation expense by reference to the level of normal annual contributions. The Special Rules regarding this aspect of allowable expenditure by the company are to be found in the SFO Practice Notes IR12/79 (para. 5.4).

If the special contributions are excessive, the SFO allow them to be spread over a number of tax periods, up to five years. The company thereby has a contingent liability for the unfunded instalments.

The view can be taken that disclosure of these contingent liabilities is important for both existing and prospective shareholders so that the effect of these costs on the company profitability can be accurately shown.

12.5 Conclusion

It is remarkable how well pension trustee boards and parent company managements have succeeded in establishing an easy, efficient working relationship in practice.

The extent to which this good relationship is achieved will depend in large measure on the knowledge and wisdom of the chairman of the trustees. Continuity is essential and there should always be a reasonable time interval before the chairman has to come for reappointment. For that reason alone, it is probably *best practice* for the chairman to be selected by the company and not left to chance and a partisan choice by the trustee board.

The other object-lesson is the importance of having some readily available means for scheme members to consult their employer company direct through Pension Advisory/Consultative Committees. Otherwise it is very difficult for the trustee board to function effectively and without a built-in sense of frustration, particularly for the member trustees.

13 Accounting, investment and membership records

The trustees of a pension scheme have a duty to the beneficiaries, i.e. the members, pensioners and deferred pensioners, to be able to account for their stewardship of the money and other assets of the scheme. There is, however, no clear legal guidance as to how they should do this or in what form accounts should be kept and presented.

Clearly, however, there is a practical need to maintain proper accounting records for a variety of reasons, including the following:

(1) Collection of contributions from members and/or their employers.
(2) Payment of insurance premiums and the making of claims, where appropriate.
(3) Prompt and accurate payment of benefits, both pensions and lump sums.
(4) Payment and reclaim of tax.
(5) Annual provision of accounts to the OPB where the scheme is contracted out, to the Inland Revenue and to the consulting actuary; and the annual certificate of solvency from the actuary to the OPB.
(6) Security and recording of invested assets and their efficient administration.
(7) Provision of information to members and others in an Annual Report (see Chapter 6).
(8) Audit and prevention of fraud.
(9) Measurement of investment performance.

13.1 Accounting records

The nature and scope of the accounting records and associated procedures will vary considerably depending upon the size and complexity of the scheme, whether the scheme administration is handled in-house or by an insurance company and/or consultants and how the fund's investments are handled. The way in which the fund's investments are handled may vary from a fully insured arrangement through funds where some or all of the investments are handled by external managers, to funds where some or even all of the investments are handled in-house.

13.1.1 *Cash book*

Regardless as to how the investments are handled, there will be a need to maintain a cash book for recording the monies paid into and out of the fund. It will also be necessary to have one or more bank accounts. As a minimum, the scheme is likely to need a current account to handle the day-to-day transactions of the scheme and a deposit account to hold fund money awaiting suitable investment opportunities or anticipated future benefit payments.

13.1.2 *Bank mandates*

Authority for signing cheques drawn on the bank accounts will either be given to the trustees or the scheme officials or a combination of both. In the interests of security, it is preferable to require all cheques to be signed by two persons. The authorities will normally be conferred by a resolution of the trustees and the bank will probably require a certified copy of the resolution.

Such bank accounts should be totally separate from the employer's in order to establish the separate status of the money as trust assets.

13.1.3 *Receipts and payment records*

All payments received by the fund such as contributions, transfer values, special funding by the employer, insurance claims and investment income should be paid into the accounts. Similarly, all benefit payments, insurance premiums, money invested and other payments by the fund should be made from the accounts. A possible exception occurs where the trustees arrange with an insurance company to pay benefits direct to the beneficiary.

13.1.4 *Banking arrangements*

It is important that no more money than is absolutely necessary for immediate needs is kept in a current bank account, and it is possible to make arrangements with the banks to transfer, automatically, any sums in excess of a set limit from the current to the deposit account. Where the sums involved are large enough, it is usual to invest the money in the money market, which can accommodate loan periods from seven days or even less up to three months or more. The longer the period for which the money is committed, the higher the rate of interest usually obtainable.

13.1.5 *Daily cash status report*

Careful watch must be maintained in order to avoid the embarrassment of a call on the fund for money when none is available. Administration procedures should, therefore, provide for regular monitoring of the receipts and payments of the scheme, notification and reconciliation of bank account balances and for forecasting future cash flows into and out of the fund.

Exceptional payments such as insurance premiums or a large lump sum benefit should be anticipated and allowed for. Where the scheme is self-invested, it will be of help to external investment fund managers to know, in advance, what money they are likely to be allocated for investment.

A simple daily cash status form is shown in Fig. 4.

Daily position at close of business on 19＿   **Current bank base rate ＿%**

	£		£
Cash book		Bank Balances	
DR		Current A/C	
CR	_____	Deposit A/C	_____
Add back unpresented cheques:–			
POST-DATED			
OTHERS _____	_____		_____
	_____		_____

Monthly position – projected

Inflow	£	*Outflow*	£
Contributions		Fund Managers	
Contributions – Special		Property Fund	
Regular Funding		Insured Managed Fund	
Transfers In		Pension Payments	
Interest		Other Fund Benefits	
Rent		Expenses	
	_____		_____
		Balance for short term investment	
	_____		_____
Property sales	_____	Investment commitments	_____

Fig. 4 Daily cash statement of monies under direct control.

13.1.6 *Ledgers*

A suitable ledger system will be necessary to record all transactions of the scheme and to enable annual accounts to be prepared and audited. Benefits paid by insurers direct should also be recorded to allow complete accounts to be prepared.

13.2 Collection of contributions

An effective method of calculating and collecting contributions is essential. Where employees contribute to the scheme they should give an authority to the employer to make the necessary deductions from their pay and pass it to the trustees. This authority is generally included in the form of application for admission to the scheme.

It is common for the overall contribution (including the employee's) to be simply expressed as a percentage of the total payroll and for the employer to pay this to the trustee's bank account. The employer then recovers the employee's share from his pay but it will involve the somewhat onerous task of reconciliation to adjust for movements to ensure that the individual contribution records are correct.

An alternative but not universally popular method is to charge the employer company the precise amount due according to the actual number of employees at the start of each pay period.

Where pensions are paid by the employer on behalf of the scheme, a net recovery system can be applied, offsetting the pension payments which are due from the pension scheme against the remittance of the combined monthly contributions.

Contributions are usually but not always payable in advance because it is an important part of the funding process that the trustees should collect contributions promptly and invest them to earn the maximum interest. Where contributions are substantial they may be paid in monthly instalments in advance. Smaller amounts may be paid either quarterly or annually in advance. The latter is the most likely in the case of insured schemes.

The collection system must ensure that the correct contributions are collected for the correct period. For example, employees may be temporarily absent or may not be paid for a period for some reason. Depending on the rules of the scheme, contributions may be suspended or paid by the employer or the employee may have the option of paying the arrears on his return to work.

The use of computerised interface programs will enable an accurate record of contributions collected to be transferred speedily from payroll to pension records where these are themselves computerised. Similarly, in the reverse direction, the same methods can be used for crediting pension payments to the pensions payroll.

The same interface programs can be used for the periodic amendments of pensionable salaries and the consequential changes in contributions charged.

13.3 Additional voluntary contributions

The scheme may permit additional voluntary contributions by the employee and these are often invested with an insurance company or a building society unless it has been decided to keep them in a separate AVC section of the main scheme where they would not be subject to the priorities clause. It is possible to arrange for these contributions to be paid direct to the insurers or the building society to save administration but it should not be forgotten that these contributions form part of the scheme's assets.

They are, therefore, the responsibility of the trustees who must be provided with adequate details of the contributions made. Likewise the insurers/building society or the scheme itself should provide an annual AVC benefit statement for each contributor showing present accrued and future expected AVC benefits, on the basis of his current contributions.

13.4 Pension payment records

It is particularly important that monthy pensions are paid on time, that they are of the correct amount, and that the correct PAYE tax has been deducted in accordance with the pensioner's tax code. Where schemes are insured but pensions are paid by the scheme, insurers will pay pensions to the scheme gross (i.e. without deduction of tax) but a few still insist on paying net of basic rate tax. In these cases, the scheme records must contain details of these deductions so that the scheme can offset them against the tax due from the scheme under PAYE. Payment of pensions to pensioners should be straightforward and is very little different from a company payroll operation. It may even be handled by the same staff.

13.5 Accounting for insured schemes

The accounting needs of insured schemes are likely to be simpler than for self-administered schemes and will vary to some extent according to the level of administration provided by the insurance company. Where the scheme is fully insured, i.e. the insurance company undertakes to provide a defined benefit in return for an agreed premium and to handle all the necessary administrative services, it may only be necessary to provide for and record the prompt payment of the premiums. The insurance company will pay the benefits, keep the records and provide summarised information for the scheme accounts.

13.5.1 *Controlled funding records*

Where systems such as controlled funding are employed, more detailed records may be necessary in order to monitor the level of funding which has been achieved and/or the benefits which have been secured from time to time. Again, it is usual for the insurers to provide detailed information annually in this respect to the scheme and the main requirement is to make sure that premiums are paid on time to ensure that cover is maintained and that claims for benefit payment are made on the insurers promptly and are dealt with by them equally promptly.

13.5.2 *Transfers of benefits to and from the scheme*

If benefits such as pensions, refunds of contributions and lump sums on death or retirement are paid in the first instance to the scheme, more detailed records of these transactions must be kept so that correct and prompt payment is made to the beneficiaries, and accounted for in the year-end accounts, and that benefits due are claimed from and paid in a timely manner by the insurers.

13.5.3 *Insurance-managed funds*

A further kind of insurance arrangement offered by many insurance companies is known as a managed fund. This is really not an insurance scheme at all but simply a kind of pooled investment vehicle permitting many small schemes to benefit from the insurance company's investment expertise and to share the risks and benefits of having their own investments by pooling their money in one or more funds specialising in different types of investment. They are more properly considered as self-administered arrangements.

13.6 Self-administered schemes

The main difference between self-administered and insured schemes is the need in the case of the former to keep detailed records of members' contributions and benefit entitlements so that correct benefits can be calculated and paid when members retire, die or leave the employer's service. In addition, more detailed investment records will be required for a self-administered scheme, unless the trustees decide to invest the scheme's assets in a single investment such as an insurance-company-managed fund. Investment records are dealt with in more detail later.

13.6.1 *Books of account*

The scheme administration will need the usual cash book, bank accounts and ledgers referred to earlier which should be capable of providing the information for the year-end accounts. Where the scheme is contracted out, it will also be necessary to account to the DHSS for the Contributions Equivalent Premiums payable in respect of employees leaving service, where appropriate, and other premiums required in certain cases such as Limited Revaluation Premiums.

13.6.2 *OPB requirements*

A further requirement for contracted-out schemes is the completion and return of Form OP21 to the OPB each year, together with the annual accounts. The purpose of this requirement is to satisfy the OPB that the correct contributions have been paid.

13.7 Investment records

The manner of investment and the related record-keeping and administration can vary considerably from scheme to scheme. Investments may comprise any combination of Stock Exchange securities (United Kingdom and overseas), unit trust investments, insurance-company-managed fund investments, insurance policies, direct property holdings, etc.

The basic need for all schemes is, however, to control effectively all existing investments and to provide for future investments in relation to the scheme's cash flow. The appropriate level of administration and record-keeping will be required although, in practice, much of this may be carried out on behalf of the trustees, if they wish, by external investment fund managers (see Chapter 10). Alternatively, the trustees may prefer to keep full records in addition to those kept by the managers, and use one of the computerised investment systems which can be incorporated into the scheme accounts (see also 13.7.2).

13.7.1 *Custody of documents*

One of the first priorities of an investment record system is to provide for safe custody of the documents of title such as insurance policies, share certificates, deposit receipts and title deeds to property. Often the services of a bank are used to provide safe custody or if external investment fund managers are used, they may provide a custodian service. In these cases, the safe custody receipts or other evidence of the securities held must themselves be kept safely. Where securities are held by third parties such as a bank, provision for quick and early access to them must be made.

13.7.2 *Contents of investment records*

For efficient management, comprehensive records are essential and they must be both accurate and kept up to date. These records must include the following:
(1) Details of each investment made showing amount, when purchased, price paid, and such other information as will provide for:
    (a) security of the investment;
    (b) prompt payment/collection of money due by or to the fund;
    (c) performance evaluation of the investment.
(2) Historical information on monies from different sources and historical outgo.
(3) Commitments already made.

(4) Forecasts of cash flows into and out of the fund.
(5) Annual audit.

13.7.3 *Management of direct investments*

Where portfolios of direct investments in quoted Stock Exchange securities are held by the fund, regular information must be obtained on stock market movements, dividend announcements, annual and interim company reports, new issues, rights issues, mergers and many other items if the investments are to be managed effectively. Direct investment should not be treated as a part-time activity. This subject is covered more fully in Chapter 10.

The ability to buy and sell investments quickly is important and there must be a system for handling the post-dealing procedures such as contract notes, stock transfer forms and payment on Stock Exchange settlement dates.

Dividends will be received net of tax which must be reclaimed from the inspector of taxes on a regular basis. This can be done monthly by agreement with the local inspector of taxes who deals with the scheme accounts.

13.7.4 *Property investments*

Funds which have direct investments in property will need detailed records of each property together with a system for dealing with rents due, demanded, paid and unpaid (and action taken). Rent reviews must be monitored and increased in line with regular valuations of the property. Tenants are often required to pay insurance premiums in addition to paying for regular maintenance and repairs. An efficient system must be maintained to ensure that the tenants comply with their obligations.

13.8 Tax payments and repayments

Schemes which are exempt approved pension schemes under FA 1970, Part II, Chapter II are not subject to income or capital gains tax on their investments. Trustees are, however, required to pay tax to and reclaim tax from the Inland Revenue in a number of circumstances and effective records must be kept to ensure prompt and accurate settlement. Some examples of cases in which tax must be paid to the Inland Revenue are given below. Tax must be paid on the following:
(1) refunds of contributions to members leaving service where tax at 10% is payable;
(2) pensions paid to members and their dependants which must be subject to deduction of tax under the PAYE system;
(3) small pensions (currently up to £104 per annum) which are commuted for a cash sum;

(4) 100% commutation of pension where the member retires on the grounds of serious ill-health.

The tax payments under (1), (3) and (4) above are often made as part of a year-end tax return, but tax due under PAYE must usually be settled monthly. At the year end, provision must be made for forms P14 to be submitted to the DHSS and the tax office and for the third copy, headed form P60, to be issued to the pensioners themselves.

Where the scheme is insured and the insurers have undertaken to pay pensions direct to pensioners on behalf of the trustees, the insurance company must account direct to the Inland Revenue for the tax deducted.

Tax deducted from dividends should be reclaimed on a regular basis, if possible monthly, in which case the inspector will probably wish to offset against these reclaims the tax due to him on contribution refunds, etc.

13.9 Year end accounts, auditing and actuarial valuations

As stated at the beginning of this chapter, there is no clear guidance on the contents and presentation of accounts for pension funds. At the time of writing, a study of the subject is being undertaken by the Accounting Standards Committee (ASC) of the principal accounting bodies, which issued a discussion paper for comments by the end of 1982. The ASC are to consider whether the comments received as a result of the discussion paper will lead to an exposure draft of a statement of accounting practice or to guidance notes or some other course.

Further study of the subject has been undertaken by the Pensions Research Accountants Group (PRAG). Their study resulted in the publication of Notes on Pensions No. 6 and No. 10, published by the NAPF in 1978 and 1981 respectively, as discussion documents. The recent discussion document issued in March 1984 by the DHSS contains proposals of far-reaching effect for pension fund accounts.

13.9.1 *Pension Fund Balance Sheet*

The principal problem covered by the research of PRAG and the NAPF has been that the preparation of a balance sheet purporting to show the assets and liabilities does not give a complete picture of the fund. This is because it does not include any information about the long-term liabilities of the fund, which are the subject of the actuarial valuations.

The accountant's balance sheet of a pension scheme should more properly be called a 'Net Asset Statement' since it is mainly designed to show the present assets with comparatives for the previous year. This should be accompanied by notes explaining the main items and by an income and expenditure account which should contain details of contributions and income received, benefits and other items paid out and adjustments in the value of the investments due to sales, purchases and market movements.

In the case of insured schemes, it may be difficult to incorporate the accrued value of the insured contract into the balance sheet. The treatment recommended by PRAG and likely to be followed by the ASC is to have an actuarial value computed by the scheme's actuary at regular intervals and to adjust this on an interim basis between valuations to reflect premiums paid and claims made.

The exact format of the accounts will depend on the nature of the scheme but a model set of accounts is set out in Appendix 8.

13.9.2 *Audit requirements*

The audit requirements of a pension scheme are similarly not well defined and will vary from scheme to scheme (and possibly from auditor to auditor). The Inland Revenue will normally require a set of audited accounts annually but the form they should take will be a matter of agreement between the trustees and the inspector of taxes.

The NAPF Notes on Pensions No. 6 referred to earlier gives a list of recommended work necessary for auditors to carry out in order to satisfy the trustees, the Inland Revenue, the employer and the members that the scheme is being properly managed. Many auditors already follow the principles on the list, or similar ones, and it can be expected that all schemes will have to comply with any accounting standard that results from the current ASC study.

13.9.3 *Actuarial valuation requirements*

Information about the cash flows and investments of the scheme is also needed for actuarial valuation purposes. Provided adequate year-end accounts together with details of the actual investments held are readily available, this requirement should present no difficulty.

It is now accepted *best practice* that an actuarial statement should be included in every Annual Report by the trustees as part of the accounts, whether or not a full valuation of the fund has taken place in the preceding year. A detailed consideration of this subject from the point of view of the consulting actuary has been given in Chapter 8.

Previously, triennial valuations were deemed sufficient, but with the computer facilities now available, more frequent valuations may become the norm, with the consulting actuary providing intervaluation certificates as to the adequacy of the cover for accrued benefits.

13.10 Membership records

As well as their duty to the members to be able to account for the assets of the scheme, the trustees have a duty to ensure that the members and their dependants receive the benefits to which they are entitled in the circumstances set out in the trust deed and rules. Equally, they must ensure that benefits in excess of the member's entitlement are not paid out.

It is therefore essential that up-to-date and accurate records are maintained for each member. An example of such a record is shown in Appendix 4, which embodies most of the basic information. The latest systems now under development have on-line facilities and can incorporate a much wider range of information.

Where the number of employees is small and/or the records required are simple, a manual record will be adequate and is to be preferred. Modern pension schemes are, however, becoming exceedingly complex, requiring more complex records and calculations. This has led an increasing number of schemes to turn to computer systems to assist them in effective administration.

13.11 Computerised record systems

The principal aims of a computer system are therefore:
(1) To perform tasks more cheaply, faster, and more accurately than at present.
(2) To provide information and/or work not possible at present.

13.11.1 *Systems available*

There is now a wide range of systems to choose from covering the following aspects of pension scheme administration:
(1) *Nominal ledger and cash book accounting.* This would not normally have a high priority because of the relatively straightforward nature of accounting transactions for a pension scheme, unless investment records were maintained in-house, as for a self-administered scheme.
(2) *Pensioner payroll.* This may be an extension of the standard payroll system in use by the employer company who might prefer to retain it under their own control, or it might be operated by the pension scheme itself.
(3) *Investment records.* Systems are readily available from a number of reputable external bureaux specialising in this field. They are of particular help in controlling investment cash flow and providing the basis for investment performance measurement. It is unlikely that it would be cost effective for a sufficiently comprehensive system to be developed from in-house resources.
(4) *Membership records and contribution accounting.* This is probably the most important aspect of pension scheme administration which derives readily identifiable benefits from the use of the appropriate computerised systems. A more detailed consideration of the problems involved in the choice of a membership record system is set out below.

13.11.2 *Membership record systems*

Up until the 1980s, it was still possible to consider a choice between using the mainframe computer facilities, operated either by the employer company or an external bureau, and using a minicomputer installed in-house, but dependent upon the mainframe to offer the complete range of services required.

The rapid development of the microcomputer in recent years and the increasing availability of compatible ancillary facilities has now made the choice far less difficult. Indeed, on grounds of cost and reliability, there is very little option now but to go straight towards the installation of a minicomputer or microcomputer dedicated to the pension scheme using one of a number of reliable and flexible software packages now available. The previous use of the in-house mainframe facility generally meant expensive and time-consuming development of a one-off specialised program to accommodate the particular needs of the company pension plan. The complexity of the interrelated sub-programs often increased as statutory changes occurred following contracting out in 1978 with a consequent increase in cost as new programs had to be developed.

The end-result has been a willingness by pension managers to accept package programs which will be regularly updated by the software supplier to accommodate any further or consequential statutory changes; even at the cost of some restriction of the bespoke additions for special features in the individual scheme.

The final choice of computerised membership record system would now appear to lie between the two following options:
(1) The development of an in-house special one-off suite of programs or the purchase of a package system on the market for use on a mainframe computer.
(2) The use of an in-house microcomputer facility with appropriate package software or a similar system operated by an outside bureau.

There are certain possible disadvantages in the use of microcomputers, such as compatibility and integration with existing systems, which should be carefully considered before making the final choice. The prospective user would be well advised to use an independent professional computer consultant for help at this stage. This arrangement will also be of value when the new facility is installed, unless an in-house systems manager for the pensions department is available.

13.11.3 *Operational problems of computerised systems*

The main problem is to secure the continuation of ongoing back-up facilities if the decision has been made to buy in a package system. Collaboration with other existing users of the system is strongly advised.

Further development such as the introduction of VDU equipment or the introduction of a multi on-line facility for sub-pension office input must always be contemplated in the design of the original in-house computer facility. Likewise, the existence of a technical link on a satellite basis with the employer company's own mainframe installation will enable the most economical use to be made of interface facilities with the payroll and personnel systems.

Any requirement for bespoke developments to a package system to accommodate the specialised requirements of a particular system will prove expensive and should be avoided wherever possible. The move to a bought-in software system provides a good opportunity to modernise your pension plan and exclude historical anomalies.

Once a system has been installed, particular attention should be paid to maintaining accurate and up-to-date data on the system, otherwise much of the advantage of computerisation will be lost. Modern computers and their software programs are very reliable but remain prone to human error.

For further and more detailed background to this subject the reader is recommended to read *Computers and Pensions in the 1980s*, a conference paper presented to the Pensions Management Institute in 1980.

13.12 Conclusion

The effective administration of a pension scheme requires sound, up-to-date accounting procedures and records, including member records. It is important, therefore, that adequate resources are provided to carry out the functions and that the functions are carried out with the care and attention they warrant.

14 Director-controlled pension schemes

In this chapter, 'director-controlled pension scheme' is taken to mean a pension scheme established by a company for its directors, either alone or with other company employees, which is not wholly insured, and of which the director members, or some of them, make up a majority of the trustees, and can thus control the investment of the scheme funds.

The company establishing the scheme is generally a private company. Such a scheme is almost always within the definition of 'small self-administered scheme', the term used by the Inland Revenue and most pension practitioners to describe a self-administered scheme with fewer than 12 members, and this chapter is written on the assumption that the scheme is subject to all the Inland Revenue requirements set out in OPB Joint Office Memorandum No. 58 for such 'small' schemes.

From the viewpoint of investment policy, a director-controlled pension scheme can fall into one of three sub-categories, as follows:

(1) A wholly self-administered scheme, avoiding all investment in insurance contracts other than term life policies for the purpose of securing death-in-service benefits only.

(2) A scheme which invests at least one-half of its money in insurance contracts, but can choose to invest the remainder in as wide a range of investments as any other self-administered scheme.

(3) A scheme which applies all its contributions as premiums on insurance contracts, on terms giving the trustees the right to obtain a loan from the insurance company on the security of those contracts; the trustees in turn lend the money so obtained to the employer company.

Apart from the three types of scheme mentioned above, there are other insured schemes, commonly called 'Executive Pension Plans', which are set up in the expectation that the insurance company concerned will make loans, on application, *direct* to the employer company, or, more frequently, to the director members of the scheme whose lives are assured. Such loans are not secured on the scheme policies, and the money advanced is not part of the scheme funds held by the trustees. The schemes are, therefore, not self-administered schemes, and are not within the scope of this chapter.

14.1 The origin of director-controlled schemes

From 1947 to 1973, a controlling director[1] could not be admitted as a member of any pension arrangement approved by the Inland Revenue, and the development of the director-controlling pension scheme was a consequence of the repeal of this prohibition by FA 1973 section 15.

There is probably an interesting story behind section 15. The government had already decided on legislation to make all company directors Class 1 contributors under the National Insurance scheme and to abolish the option open to some directors to be treated as self-employed persons. This would have made all directors liable to participate in the earnings-related part of the new State pension scheme introduced by the SSPA 1975. At the same time, the government were anxious to encourage contracting out of the new scheme through membership of 'recognised' occupational pension schemes. The Inland Revenue were, therefore, bound to allow even controlling directors to participate to some extent in schemes seeking 'recognition', if they wished to contract out. But it caused some surprise that the Inland Revenue went as far as they did in tabling in the Finance Bill a complete repeal of the old prohibition, with no strings attached. Did they underestimate the number of controlling directors? In the event, the repeal led to the creation of a flood of schemes for directors in the formerly prohibited category, the majority being wholly insured. But a significant number of companies have since chosen to set up self-administered schemes.

At first the motive was generally said to be the hope of a higher yield from direct investment than was being offered at the time on short-term insurance contracts ('short term', because most of the individuals to be assured were in their fifties or sixties). Later it became evident that the attraction was often the opportunity available under self-administered schemes to invest at least part of the fund in, or for the benefit of, the employer company itself rather than in government securities or quoted shares.

---

[1] According to FA 1970 section 26, a controlling director is 'a director of a company, the directors whereof have a controlling interest therein, who is the beneficial owner of, or able either directly or through the medium of other companies or by any other means to control, more than five per cent of the ordinary share capital of the company'.

14.2 The attitude of the Inland Revenue to director-controlled schemes

14.2.1 *Self-administered schemes for directors*

At first, the Inland Revenue were firmly opposed to the approval of a self-administered scheme for only a few individuals – particularly directors of family companies – on the grounds that such a scheme would be 'unstable'. By this the Inland Revenue meant that, although the scheme would be established under ostensibly irrevocable trusts, there was a risk that after the tax advantages arising from approval had been enjoyed for perhaps many years, the scheme would be summarily terminated and the assets shared out among the members and their dependants.

Although this would be a breach of trust (because the consent of literally *all* the persons beneficially interested would be unobtainable), it was felt that a situation could easily result in which no one was disposed to take legal action to counter it. The risk would be particularly great if the employer company had itself fallen on bad days and the pension scheme money was needed to support it.

14.2.2 *Restriction on number of schemes*

The Inland Revenue will approve, for each employer-company, only one small self-administered scheme of the kind described in this chapter, and which is subject to the special requirements covered in para. 14.5 below. They do not consider that different levels of benefit or differences of view among the members about the investment of scheme funds justify the company setting up two or more separate schemes in this category.

However, the Inland Revenue will not object to the creation of two separate small self-administered schemes, one for directors, or employees belonging to the controlling family, and the other for 'rank and file' employees, where the members of the second scheme, although fewer than 12 in number, are at arm's length from each other, from the company and from the trustees, so that the scheme can be exempted from the special requirements.

14.2.3 *Pensioneer trustees*

The Inland Revenue had a weapon to discourage such action in the form of FA 1971 paragraph 9, Schedule 3, which provides for a tax assessment on any *employee* to whom, or for whose benefit, any unauthorised lump sum is paid out of pension scheme funds, but evidently the Inland Revenue did not regard this as an adequate deterrent to the improper termination of schemes which they feared.

However, the apparent impasse was resolved when the Inland Revenue accepted the concept of 'pensioneer trustees' coupled with the requirement to purchase annuities (see 14.5 below).

14.3 Advantages of director-controlled pension schemes

As the definition at the start of this chapter indicates, the director members of the pension scheme will form a majority of the trustees and be able to determine the policy governing the investment of the scheme funds, if they wish to do so. They will probably regard the main benefit from this power as the ability it confers to use the scheme funds to develop the business of the employer company rather than to invest them elsewhere. There are various ways in which this can be done, which are as follows:

(1) By making loans to the company.
(2) By subscribing for shares in the company.
(3) By purchasing commercial property and leasing it to the company.

There are some differences of opinion among pension practitioners about the prudence of such a policy. Some take the view that the best method of providing good pensions for directors is to use the money set aside in the area in which the directors are most knowledgeable, i.e. in their own companies' business. Money ploughed back will produce greater profits to finance greater pension contributions, and higher yields on such contributions, with bigger pensions at the end of the day. The opposite school of thought quotes the adage concerning 'too many eggs in one basket' and stresses the undeniable truth that insolvency of the company could lead to loss of both livelihood and the funds for financial support in old age.

But whether or not directors consider it wise to invest pension scheme monies in their own company in the long term, it is certainly worth considering loans back to the company at a time of temporary cash shortage when the company might otherwise have to suspend or reduce contributions to a pension scheme investing wholly in insurance contracts or arm's length securities. A survey in *Pensions Monthly* showed that only a relatively small percentage (10%) made loans back to their own companies.

For example, if the recommended rate of company contribution to a directors' scheme is £50,000 per annum, attracting relief from corporation tax at, say, 30%, the net cost of contribution is £35,000. But this outflow of company cash can be reduced to a mere £10,000 by lending back one-half of the gross contribution, i.e. £25,000.

14.4 Essential prerequisite planning

A discussion of the practicabilities of establishing and running a director-controlled pension scheme should cover three aspects:

(1) The things that must be done.
(2) The things that may be done and the conditions to be observed.
(3) The things that must not be done.

14.4.1 *Pensioneer trustees*

It is mandatory if a director-controlled pension scheme is to be approved by the Inland Revenue that the trustees appointed must include a 'pensioneer trustee' recognised by the Inland Revenue, i.e. a professional man (he may be an actuary, a senior employee of a life office or a consultant) widely involved with occupational pension schemes who has given the Inland Revenue an undertaking that he will not consent to the termination of any scheme of which he is a trustee, otherwise than in accordance with the terms of the relevant approved rules. In short, he must be a man on whom the Inland Revenue can rely to block any attempt by the other trustees, or the members, to act as described in 14.2.1 above.[2]

Many corporate bodies which are controlled by individual directors satisfying the criteria are also accepted as pensioneer trustees.

To prevent a pensioneer trustee being overruled by a majority decision of the other trustees, the trust deed must require a unanimous decision of all trustees if the scheme is to be terminated. On all other matters, the pensioneer trustee has no greater power than any other trustee.

14.5 Revenue requirements

Another mandatory requirement is that at the time when any pension becomes payable, or within a specified period of grace thereafter, the trustees must secure their liability by purchasing an annuity from a life office equal to the pension they have to pay, including any pension increases already awarded.

This requirement stems primarily from the Inland Revenue's preoccupation with the case of *Saunders* v. *Vautier* mentioned in the footnote to 14.4.1 above, and the situation described in this footnote is indeed more likely to exist after all the scheme members have retired when they, together with their surviving wives, may become the only persons with an interest under the trusts.

The purchase of an annuity does not reduce their rights to bring the trust to an end, but simply puts most of the scheme money out of their reach if they do so.

If, under the scheme rules, a pension is not guaranteed to be payable for a minimum period (which may extend beyond the pensioner's death), a life office annuity must be purchased immediately at pension commencement date. Otherwise, the period of grace corresponds with the guarantee period, which is normally either five or ten years.

However, from the practical viewpoint, the obligation of the trustees to

---

[2] In a situation where *all* the persons with interests under a trust, being adults and free of any legal disability, determine to bring the trust to an end, no one has the power to prevent their doing so – see *Saunders* v. *Vautier* (1841). But this situation is very unlikely to exist in the context of a conventional pension scheme, and is not the situation against which the presence of a pensioneer trustee is intended to safeguard the Inland Revenue.

secure pensions by buying life office annuities is of greater value to the scheme members than it is to the Inland Revenue. A scheme with only a handful of members is not big enough to carry the mortality risks itself. If its funds have been built up on an assumption that each member has a normal life expectancy, the scheme will become insolvent if – and this is not impossible with very small numbers – a majority of the members survive to age 85 or 90.

So the mortality risks must be spread over a much wider group of lives, within which the 'swings and roundabouts' principle is sure to operate, so that all pensioners may have proper security for their benefits.

Even after the trustees have bought an annuity in respect of a pensioner, they may continue to hold funds with which to finance further pension increases they may need to grant to offset future rises in the cost of living.

14.6 The provision of death benefit cover

A pension scheme with few members should also not attempt to carry the mortality risks of death-in-service, if the benefit payable in that contingency is a lump sum representing a multiple of the deceased's previous remuneration, or if dependants' pensions are being provided. A term life policy will need to be taken out to secure the estimated excess cost of the benefit payable under the rules over the current value of the member's interest in the fund (the amount accumulated to meet the cost of his accrued pension and post-retirement dependants' benefits).

14.7 The facility for trustees to lend back to employer

It has already been mentioned above that it is possible for the trustees to lend money to the employer company. The Inland Revenue have not taken sides in the differences of view among practitioners about the advisability of this type of investment. Nevertheless, for reasons of their own, they impose a limit, that is, that such loans should not exceed one-half of the value of the scheme funds. If the scheme trustees also hold shares in the employer company, the one-half limit applies to the aggregate value of both shares and loans taken together.

14.7.1 Relaxation of loan limit

The one-half limit for loans can perhaps be exceeded if a scheme originally established as an Executive Pension Plan of the kind mentioned at the start of this chapter is converted into a director-controlled pension scheme with direct investment, on the entry of new members, or if there is scope for a large increase in the level of benefits for existing members. Let us suppose that after a few years, the financial position of the scheme is as follows:

	£
Stock Exchange investments	120,000
Original Executive Pension Plan policy (surrender value)	40,000
	£160,000

Sufficient of the investments can be realised to make £80,000 available as a loan from the trustees to the employer company, while the member to whom the Executive Pension Plan policy relates can take a personal loan from the life office, if the office is still prepared to allow this facility.

14.7.2 Security for loanback

The Inland Revenue leave it to the trustees to decide whether loans to the employer company should be secured or not. If the investment powers of the trustees are sufficiently widely drawn in the trust deed, e.g. 'in any form of investment which they could make if they were absolutely and beneficially entitled thereto and also to lend with or without security', an unsecured loan would not be *ultra vires*.

But it does not follow that such an investment is one which the trustees should make, acting with the prudence that is expected of them; if the company becomes insolvent, and all or part of the money lent is lost, to the detriment of the retirement benefits payable under the scheme, it is not impossible that the trustees will be faced with an action for misfeasance, initiated by a scheme member who was not a trustee when the loan was made, or by a dependant of a member.

14.7.3 Documentation of loanback

The Inland Revenue require that any loan made by the trustees to the employer company should be on commercial terms as if the parties were at arm's length. This means that there must be either a formal loan agreement, or, as a minimum, a written memorandum recording the existence of the loan, the arrangements governing repayment and the rate of interest.

The rate of interest must also be a commercial one, which will, of course, depend on all the circumstances, e.g. whether the loan is secured or unsecured, its duration and whether the interest rate is fixed or fluctuating. The Inland Revenue have expressed the view that 3% above Clearing Bank Base Rate would be a reasonable fluctuating rate on an unsecured loan.

14.8 Investment of fund in employer company

As regards investment in the share capital of the employer company, it should be borne in mind that any acquisition of shares by the trustees is a 'transaction in securities', a term used in the Income and Corporation Taxes Act 1970 section 460.

This section contains wide-ranging provisions to counter tax avoidance and needs to be heeded by trustees and the members of schemes before any transfer of shares between them is put in hand. For example, the Inland Revenue (Technical Division) have taken the view that a purchase of shares for cash by scheme trustees from a company employee who is a member of the scheme gives rise to a 'tax advantage' on the part of the vendor which they can counteract by invoking section 460.

It is desirable, therefore, that the parties should seek a clearance from the Inland Revenue – as they are entitled to do by section 464 – before committing themselves to any 'transaction in securities' between themselves. If it is intended that the scheme should acquire shares in the employer company, a straightforward cash subscription for newly issued shares is probably the most advisable method of doing so.

14.9 Property investment

Many director-controlled pension schemes invest part of their funds in commercial property. This may sometimes be tenanted property bought by the trustees from a third party which has no connection with the trade of the employer company.

But frequently director trustees decided to 'kill two birds with one stone' and to buy property either (a) from a third party but to be made available for use by the employer company, or (b) from the employer company itself, with provision for a lease back to that company. In the latter case, the purpose will be to allow the company to realise the value of its property without losing the use of it, and to obtain cash for working capital or to finance business development.

14.9.1 Trustee attitude to property investment

In a property transaction involving the employer company, whether it is a purchase from the company or merely a lease of property to the company at a rent, it is essential when the terms of the transaction are being settled that the trustees of the scheme should act as if the company were a stranger at arm's length.

One of the conditions for tax approval of a scheme to which the Inland Revenue attach great importance is that the scheme must be 'bona fide established for the sole purpose of providing relevant benefits' (FA 1970 section 19 (2)(a)). When the trustees of a scheme decide to buy property from the employer company, it is perfectly clear that in truth they have a dual purpose: they wish to make an investment for the scheme, and to do something useful for the company's business.

They would not be human if they were not conscious of their other function as company directors. However, it is unlikely that the Inland Revenue will regard a transaction as incompatible with the 'sole purpose' condition if the property or lease acquired is in every way a good investment on its own merits, and an investment which could just as well have been made by trustees who were in no way connected with the employer company.

So it is necessary for the trustees to obtain a professional valuation of any property bought, and professional advice about the proper rent to charge the company, and to follow that advice. They may feel a natural reluctance to spend money on professional fees on the grounds that the company and the scheme are so closely connected that a few thousand pounds either way is 'neither here nor there', but the Inland Revenue will not accept this approach.

14.9.2 *Possible prejudice of Revenue approval for property purchases*

There are two circumstances where the Inland Revenue would probably regard a property purchase as prejudicing the approval of the scheme.

The first of these circumstances involves the situation whereby the transaction requires the trustees to borrow a lot of money – and in this context 'a lot of money' means more than about three years' ordinary annual contributions to the scheme. Thus, it would probably be satisfactory for a scheme receiving an annual contribution of £100,000 to buy a property for £450,000 with a down-payment of £150,000 and a mortgage loan of £300,000.

But if the annual contribution were only £50,000, the Inland Revenue would probably object to the trustees borrowing £300,000. This seemingly anomalous view is also based on the 'sole purpose' condition mentioned above. Trustees solely concerned with providing retirement and death benefits would probably be content to invest merely the money coming into the scheme for investment, and would not seek to buy a property costing far more than the funds available, and requiring borrowing.

If trustees do engage in such a transaction, they must have some motive other than the straightforward provision of relevant benefits, and if the employer company is the other party to the transaction, and will benefit from it one way or another, it is easy to see what the other motive is. However, in practice the Inland Revenue will not use this argument against modest borrowing, i.e. up to three years' annual contributions.

In the second circumstance, the trustees must make sure that they do not tie up in commercial property money which they will need to use in purchasing a life office annuity at or soon after the retirement of a member (see 14.5 above). There are no 'rules of thumb' here and trustees must be guided by common sense in the light of all the circumstances. If the scheme has literally only one member, there is no escape from the need to realise the bulk of the fund when he retires, and it would be pointless to invest most of it in property only five years before normal pension age. But the same investment would be unobjectionable if the member had 20 years' service in front of him.

There would be ample time to plan, for example, for the employer company to acquire or reacquire ownership of the property in the interim. At the other extreme, a scheme with eight members of widely differing ages – and the likelihood of new entrants – could happily invest 75% of its fund in a property, and plan to retain it as a long-term investment, in the knowledge that successive well-spaced retirements could probably be financed mainly out of future contribution income.

The Inland Revenue take an interest in this subject and are likely to react adversely if the trustees appear to be behaving in an unpractical way and creating a potential liquidity problem for themselves.

14.10 Revenue prohibitions

14.10.1 *General attitude of the Revenue*

We now come to the things that must not be done if tax approval by the Inland Revenue is to be retained. Basically, the Revenue are concerned that an approved scheme should not be used to provide any kind of financial benefit or advantage for its members while they are still in service, and all the prohibitions stem from this principle.

14.10.2 *Lending to members*

First, the scheme must not lend money, even at a commercial rate of interest, to its members, or their dependants, and this caveat must actually be written into the clauses of the trust deed giving the trustees their investment powers.

14.10.3 *Fine art investments*

Secondly, the scheme must not invest money in yachts, jewellery, works of art, or other valuable chattels which could be made available for the members' personal use. There are probably political considerations here and the Revenue no doubt wish to avoid any possibility of an embarrassing parliamentary row following publicity about the use of tax-exempt funds to enhance the lifestyle of certain company directors.

Arguments that assets of that kind may be a good investment because of capital appreciation, and that it is well known that the British Rail Pension Fund has invested in old masters, will fall on deaf ears. It is unlikely that the driver of an Inter-City train, or even the Chairman of British Rail himself, is allowed to hang them in his dining-room.

14.10.4 *Investments in residential property*

Thirdly, there is general opposition on the part of the Revenue to investment in residential property, or farming land, with vacant possession, so that the property in question could be made available for occupation by members of the scheme. The purchase of a block of flats already occupied by secure tenants, and producing a good rental income, would be unobjectionable.

14.11 Actuarial requirements

All self-administered schemes run by large employers, except some operating on a money purchase basis, have used, as a matter of course, the services of an actuary to determine the rate of contributions required, and to review the fund periodically.

In relation to director-controlled pension schemes, however, the Inland Revenue have made it a positive requirement for approval that there must be an actuarial report at the outset to set the rate of contribution, and actuarial valuations thereafter at least every three years.

Presumably, the Revenue fear that the trustees of a small scheme for a handful of members may be tempted to save professional fees and adopt a 'do-it-yourself' approach to funding calculations.

In the same context, the Inland Revenue have also broken with tradition, i.e. not to intervene in any way with the exercise of an actuary's professional judgement, and have made it clear that they will not necessarily accept funding calculations unless based on assumptions of certain minimum investment yields.

One can understand the reasons for the Revenue's attitude. The large public company running a scheme for hundreds of ordinary employees will certainly not wish to contribute more than it has to, while the directors of a private company may wish to minimise taxable profits by putting into the tax haven of their own pension scheme as much as they can get away with.

It would be pointless for the Inland Revenue to seek to control tax relief by setting limits on the emerging benefits, but not to concern themselves with the calculation of the contributions made to secure those benefits.

Thus, the Inland Revenue will expect the actuary to assume a net yield during the directors' service of at least 0.5% (i.e. that the average gross investment yield will exceed the rate of salary progression by 0.5% or more), and a net yield after retirement of at least 2% (i.e. that the gross investment yield will exceed the average rate of increase in the Retail Price Index by 2% or more, per year).

14.12 Conclusion

There can be no doubt that the repeal of the prohibition in FA 1973 section 15 concerning controlling directors has been the most significant relaxation affecting a particular class of employees which has occurred in the pensions industry for many years.

Even though the original motives behind the repeal flowed from a much more lowly desire on the part of the government to tidy up National Insurance contributions for company directors in advance of an anticipated new State pension scheme, the benefits have nonetheless been very real.

The market was slow to respond to the potential thus released, but rapidly caught up and nowadays no self-respecting insurance company would be without an Executive Pension Plan among its products; while those controlling directors who prefer the money not to pass to insurance companies (either in whole or in part) have, thanks to the enlightened attitude of the SFO and the prudence of practitioners, the opportunity of going the self-administered route.

The development and control of director-controlled pension schemes have been in keeping with the practice with which the occupational pensions industry had justly earned a high reputation, in spite of fears of abuse expressed in the media. It has been necessary to tighten the practice screw a little here and relax it a little there, but there has been very little evidence of actual malpractice.

If one believes that small companies and their successful development could be the lifeblood of future economic prosperity and enhanced employment prospects, director-controlled pension schemes will have made a small but nevertheless significant contribution to that desirable objective.

15 Statutory responsibilities of pension scheme administrators, trustees and employers

There is no statutory obligation under United Kingdom law for a company to set up an occupational pension scheme for its employees. However, once a company has decided to do so, statutory obligations arise under three Acts of Parliament and the subsequent statutory amendments and regulations. The three Acts are as follows:

(1) *Finance Act 1970* (FA 1970). This provides valuable tax concessions for the company, for employees who are members of the pension scheme and for the pension scheme itself.

(2) *Social Security Act 1973* (SSA 1973). This Act requires pension schemes to ensure that a member who leaves before the scheme's normal retirement age has his pension rights preserved (within certain limits).

(3) *Social Security Pensions Act 1975* (SSPA 1975). This Act permits a company to 'contract out' members of its pension scheme if it so wishes. If this option is taken up, the company and those of its employees who are scheme members pay lower National Insurance contributions than would otherwise be the case and the pension scheme accepts responsibility for providing the earnings-related part of the State pension.

FA 1970 is the responsibility of the Inland Revenue and is administered by the SFO, which is a branch of the Revenue.

The other two Acts are the responsibility of the Department of Health and Social Security, but most of the Acts' provisions are administered by the OPB, which is an independent statutory body. The offices of the SFO and the OPB are located on the same site and the two bodies work closely together. Their present address is as follows:

SFO and OPB,
Lynwood Road,
Thames Ditton,
Surrey KT7 0DP

The effect of these statutory requirements must be considered at the following stages:
(1) Before starting a contracted-out scheme.
(2) During the operation of the scheme.
(3) When the scheme closes down.

The SFO set out their requirements for approving pension schemes in the Inland Revenue's Practice Notes. The official title is 'Inland Revenue – Occupational Pension Schemes' ref. IR12 (1979). It has been reissued as OPB Joint Office Memorandum 63/79.

The OPB set out their requirements and practice in a series of memoranda. Amendments and notes on changes in practice by both the SFO and the OPB are set out in periodic 'joint' memoranda issued jointly by the SFO and the OPB.

Copies of these documents are obtainable from the OPB/SFO Joint Office. They are essential tools of the trade for pension administrators.

15.1 Statutory requirements when starting a scheme

15.1.1 *SFO*

It is essential to obtain the SFO's approval to a new scheme. A scheme that has the SFO's approval is called an 'exempt approved scheme' and this results in valuable tax concessions, which are as follows:
(1) Contributions paid into the scheme by the company are an allowable tax expense.
(2) Contributions to the scheme by employees are exempt from tax (the contributions are deducted from gross pay before tax is applied).
(3) Income from the scheme's investments is exempt from income tax and any tax deducted from investment income can be reclaimed. No capital gains tax liability arises on investment transactions.

The basic requirement of the SFO is that a pension scheme must be set up under an irrevocable trust. This is to ensure that the funds of the scheme are separate from the company's monies, so that should the company go out of business, the employee's pension rights are not put in jeopardy.

15.1.2 *Scheme administrator*

In addition, the SFO require that a scheme must have an 'administrator' who is responsible for supplying information about the scheme to the SFO. The administrator is generally the pension scheme manager. He can also be a trustee of the scheme or the employer or the Secretary of the scheme's committee of management.

Whoever is appointed as administrator must be a resident in the United Kingdom. If a company has its headquarters, including its pension administration, abroad, the SFO will not approve the scheme unless a person resident in the United Kingdom is responsible for discharging the duties of the administrator. *Best practice* is to appoint the pension scheme manager as the administrator, if such an officer is available.

15.1.3 *Documentation: trust deed and scheme rules*

Before a pension scheme can be established as an exempt approved scheme under FA 1970, the SFO require a trust deed (the definitive trust deed) and a set of scheme rules to be drawn up and submitted to them for approval. These can be separate documents or can be combined in one document.

The scheme rules must set out in exact detail the definition of membership of the scheme, the contributions to be paid by members (if any), the normal annual contributions to be paid by the company, together with provision for special contributions, the benefits to be provided and the normal retiring age. A winding-up rule must be included.

These documents set out the legal rights and obligations of both the company and the members of the scheme. Consequently, they must be meticulously drafted and normally be prepared by a solicitor specialising in trust and pension law or by a pension consultant or the insurance company if the scheme is to be an insured one. The basic layout of a model trust deed is set out in Appendix 2.

If the scheme is contracted out, the OPB have the same requirements as the SFO but only one set of documents need be sent to the SFO/OPB office.

15.1.4 *Interim trust deed*

Where the definitive trust deed cannot be executed in its final form before the date on which a new scheme is to come into operation (as is usually the case), the SFO will normally accept that the scheme is effectively established by an interim deed or declaration creating an irrevocable trust in relation to the monies or insurance policies to be held by the scheme and setting out the main purposes of the scheme. Certain specific undertakings relating to Revenue limits also have to be given by the scheme trustee.

The interim deed will enable the scheme to have 'exempt approved' status from the start. The OPB will also accept such an interim deed, preferably accompanied by a copy of the scheme rules as issued to the members, for contracting-out status. The SFO, however, will require a deed of indemnity before they will allow tax to be reclaimed on investment income of the pension fund before the definitive deed is executed.

15.1.5 *Actuarial report*

The SFO must be provided with an actuarial report from an independent actuary if the scheme is self-administered, or from the insurance company's actuary if it is insured. This is to ensure that the scheme has been properly costed and is properly funded from the start under the contracting-out regulations. Continuing actuarial certificates are required to ensure that the requisite benefits are covered and the accrued guaranteed minimum benefit is adequately secured.

15.1.6 *SFO limits*

FA 1970 places limitation on the benefits that schemes can provide. In designing a new scheme, these limits must be adhered to if exempt approved status is not to be jeopardised, and the trustees have to enter into specific undertakings to observe them. The main limits are as follows:

(1) *Benefits.* The maximum pension that a scheme may provide is 40/60ths (i.e. two thirds) of final salary, payable at the scheme's normal retirement age which may be any age between 60–70 for men and 55–70 for women. The only exception is where a member continues working after normal retirement age; in this case the maximum is 45/60th.

Normally, of course, such a pension is earned on the basis of 1/60th of final salary for each year of service up to a maximum of 40. However, late entrants to a scheme may be given 'uplifted 60ths' so that they could earn up to a 40/60ths pension after only ten years' service. The stipulation that, where an employee has a pension from a previous employer, the total of his two pensions cannot exceed 40/60ths of his final salary with his last employer, has recently been relaxed – OPB memorandum 10/82 refers.

(2) *Lump sum benefits.* On retirement, a member may be given a tax-free lump sum not exceeding 3/80ths of final salary for each year of service. This lump sum may be provided by commuting part of the pension or the scheme rules may provide a maximum pension of 40/80ths of final salary plus the lump sum. A scheme *cannot* provide a 40/60ths pension plus a lump sum. Schemes may calculate pensions on some other basis, e.g. money purchase or career average, but whatever basis is used, the maximum pension must not exceed the equivalent of two thirds of final salary.

(3) *Death benefits.* Schemes may provide pensions for both widows and widowers if they so wish (if a scheme is contracted out it *must* provide widow's pensions). The maximum pension permitted by the SFO is two thirds of the maximum pension that could have been approved

for the dead employee. In addition, a lump sum not exceeding £5,000, or if greater, four times the deceased employee's final salary, may be payable if death occurs in service.

(4) *Contributions.* The maximum annual contribution an employee may make to a pension scheme, including voluntary contributions, is now 15% of his pay – but that is subject to a flexible interpretation and can be extended to include all Schedule E earnings.

The SFO has considerable discretion to vary these limits and other aspects of the legislation.

15.2 Contracting out of State scheme

It is only necessary to submit scheme documents to, and seek approval from, the OPB if the company decides to contract out its pensionable employees from the earnings-related part of the State pension scheme.

15.2.1 *Requirements for contracting out*

If a company decides to contract out, its pension scheme must provide on retirement a pension of at least half final salary after 40 years' service, coupled with a guarantee that whatever pension was paid in relation to a period of contracted-out employment would not be less than the equivalent additional component that would have resulted from full participation in the State scheme for the same period on the same earnings. This is the Guaranteed Minimum Pension.

15.2.2 *Requisite benefits*

Under SSPA 1975, a contracted-out scheme must provide 'requisite' benefits comprising the following:

(1) *A personal pension.* A personal pension based on the member's final salary, or his average pensionable salary revalued in line with the growth in earnings. 'Pensionable salary' need not be calculated on the same earnings as those from which the GMP is calculated – e.g. bonus and/or overtime payments may be excluded as long as the OPB's approval is obtained.

   Normally, the pension must build up at a rate of not less than $1\frac{1}{4}\%$ (1/80th) of pensionable salary for each year of contracted-out service, although years of service may be limited to those necessary to produce a half-salary pension (i.e. 40 years on an 80ths scheme). The OPB has discretion to accept a lower rate of accrual than $1\frac{1}{4}\%$ as long as the scheme's overall benefits are approximately equivalent. Finally, the amount of each member's personal pension must not be less than his GMP.

(2) *A widow's pension.* A widow's pension of at least $\frac{5}{8}\%$ of her husband's final or revalued average salary (i.e. his salary at death) for each year of contracted-out employment. (Note: there is no limit to the number

of years that count in calculating a widow's pension.) The amount of the widow's pension must not be less than the Widow's GMP which is half the husband's GMP (including any increments for postponed retirement) accrued up to the end of the tax year preceding his death.

The widow's pension must be payable if the widow is entitled to a State scheme widowed mother's allowance, widow's pension or a Category B retirement pension (i.e. one based on her husband's insurance). The Widow's GMP must be paid to the legal widow but any excess of scheme widow's pension over and above the GMP may be paid to another dependant of the deceased husband, subject to scheme rules and OPB approval. (Note: under the State scheme, the widow receives her late husband's additional component in full; the Widow's GMP is only half that of her husband's GMP. The balance of additional component, after the Widow's GMP has been deducted, is paid by the State.)

In SSPA 1975, these benefits are called the 'requisite benefits' and are the minimum required. A pension scheme can provide higher benefits, e.g. 60ths, so that a member with 40 years' service receives a pension of two thirds of his final salary. It should be noted that if the scheme does provide such higher benefits, these higher benefits are its 'requisite benefits'.

15.2.3 *Rebate of contributions to State scheme*

In return, the National Insurance contributions of the company are reduced by 4.1% and those of its contracted-out employees by 2.15%, both reductions applying to earnings between £34.00 and £250 per week. These are the figures in force at October 1984, but they are adjusted as from 6 April of each year to reflect the rise in National Average Earnings.

15.2.4 *A winding-up provision*

In addition, a contracted-out scheme must give priority in its rules to the provision of the following benefits in the event of the scheme ceasing:
(1) The GMPs and accrued rights to them (on the bases for securing these liabilities approved by the OPB).
(2) EPBs provided if the scheme was contracted out under the graduated pension ('Boyd Carpenter') 1961 scheme.
(3) Pensions and other benefits in respect of which entitlement to payment had already arisen, other than those in (1) and (2) above.
(4) Any other liabilities which are given priority equal to, or greater than, that accorded to (1) to (3) above.
(5) Administration expenses which would be payable out of the resources of the scheme on winding up.

15.2.5 *Procedure for making an application to contract out*

The basis of contracting out under SSPA 1975 is that employers must take the decision to contract their employees (or certain of their employees) out of part of the State scheme. Thus, it is the employer (or employers if several of them have employees in the same scheme) who must apply formally to the OPB for a 'contracting-out certificate', even if the work is done by his pension consultants, insurance company, etc., acting as his agent. The certificate relates to employments – often in such simple terms as 'all employees of the XYZ company who are members of the XYZ pension scheme'. The reason for this is that the certificate is the employer's authority to pay reduced-rate National Insurance contributions.

15.2.6 *Notice to employees of intention to contract out*

The first step in applying for a certificate is for the employer to give at least three months' notice of his intention to do so to the following:
(1) The employees concerned (i.e. all those in the employment(s) to which the certificate will relate, even if some will not actually be contracted out).
(2) Any independent trade union recognised to any extent for the purpose of collective bargaining on behalf of those employees.
(3) The trustees and administrator of the scheme.
(4) The insurance company if the scheme's benefits are to be provided by means of an insurance policy.
  The notice must do the following:
(1) State the employer's intention to contract out.
(2) Describe the scheme benefits and any contributions which the employee has to pay to the scheme.
(3) Explain any change there will be in the scheme's benefits and employees' contributions in order to contract out.
(4) Explain the effect of contracting out on State scheme benefits and contributions (this can be done by reference to another document – the OPB will supply such a document).
(5) Give particulars of people to whom representations may be made (e.g. the personnel officer), and tell employees that representations may be made direct to the OPB up to 14 days after the notice expires.
  Notices must also be given prior to the variation or surrender of a contracting-out certificate, although the OPB have discretion to vary the requirement in these cases. Before or during this period, the employer must consult with all the recognised trade unions concerned. Once the period of notice has expired, the employer makes an 'election' to contract out to the OPB; this should be done within three months of the expiry of the notice.

15.2.7 *The election*

The election should set out the employments to be contracted out, details of the scheme, and should be accompanied by a copy of the scheme's rules, latest annual accounts and the latest actuary's report.

An employer wishing to contract out members of a scheme cannot discriminate between different employees on any grounds other than the nature of their employment except for any who will be within five years of the scheme's normal pension age when contracting-out starts. If there are both men and women in a particular employment covered by the scheme, the employer must contract out both the men and women – this is the result of the equal access provisions of SSPA 1975.

15.3 Not contracting out

In the event of the company deciding *not* to contract out, there is *no need to submit the scheme's documents* to the OPB.

15.3.1 *Preservation requirements, SSA 1973*

The scheme must, however, meet the 'preservation' requirements of SSA 1973. These are that the scheme rules provide that any member who leaves the company's employment with more than five years' pensionable service and who is over age 26 must be given pension rights he has earned, i.e. these rights cannot be extinguished by a refund of contributions. This prohibition does not necessarily extend to a refund of pre-1975 contributions if the scheme rules so permit. The member's pension rights may be provided by the following:

(1) Preserving them within the scheme, i.e. the member remains on the books of the scheme and his pension is paid to him when he reaches pensionable age.
(2) Transferring the pension rights to another pension scheme of which the person has become a member.
(3) Purchasing an annuity from an insurance company which will produce the appropriate pension at pensionable age.

If the scheme is not to be contracted out of SSPA 1975, a similar notice as that set out above for contracting out must be sent to the same people within three months of the start of the scheme.

15.4 Statutory requirements after a scheme has started

15.4.1 *SFO*

The trust deed of an exempt approved scheme commits the trustees to abiding by the SFO limits and to administering the scheme to ensure protection of the members' pension benefits. Consequently, any change in the circumstances of the company that affects the pension scheme, such as a new company joining the group of companies and participating in the pension scheme, must be reported immediately to the SFO. In particular, any change in the scheme's provisions that affect SFO limits, particularly benefits, will require amendment of the trust deed and/or the scheme's rules. Such amendments must be submitted to the SFO for their approval.

Whenever an actuarial valuation is carried out, a copy of the actuary's report must be sent to the SFO, as must copies of the scheme's report and accounts.

In addition, the administrator must provide the inspector of taxes with copies of the scheme's accounts and any other information the inspector may require in connection with the tax exempt approval of the pension scheme.

15.4.2 OPB

Once the OPB have issued a contracting-out certificate, its continuing supervision is aimed at ensuring that a scheme is able to provide GMPs in all circumstances in the future.

The Board requires copies of schemes' annual accounts but its main condition is that the scheme's actuary shall be able, from time to time, to supply them with an 'actuarial certificate' to the effect that the scheme's resources are sufficient to provide the 'priority liabilities', in particular, the scheme's GMP liability, were the scheme to be wound up in the next five years.

An actuarial certificate is required with the application for a contracting-out certificate and subsequent certificates must be provided at not more than three-and-a-half-yearly intervals.

Certificates must also be provided at the following times:
(1) When an actuarial valuation produces new circumstances which, in the actuary's opinion, invalidate the previous certificate.
(2) When any substantial alteration is made to the scheme.

The position may arise where the actuary, because of changed circumstances, may find it impossible to give a further certificate. In this event, if he thinks that the insufficiency of resources is only temporary, proposals to remedy the situation may be prepared and submitted by the employer to the OPB who will consider what action is necessary to safeguard the GMPs. The OPB may impose whatever conditions they consider necessary and failure to comply with them may result in cancellation of the contracting-out certificate.

The OPB can, if necessary, insist that the employer pays into the scheme in order to bring its resources to, and maintain them at, a satisfactory level.

The OPB and the SFO must also be informed of any alteration of scheme rules, whether the change affects contracting out or not. Above all, the OPB must be informed immediately if a scheme is to cease to contract out, is to be closed or is to be wound up.

15.4.3 *DHSS*

The OPB are responsible for ensuring that the rules of a contracted-out scheme meet the requirements of the Act for contracting out and that the scheme's finances are sufficient to meet its GMP liabilities. In other words, the OPB are concerned with the scheme as a whole.

The responsibility for monitoring the procedure whereby individual members receive their correct GMP rests with the DHSS. SSPA 1975 and the regulations made under it require that, whenever an employee leaves contracted-out employment, a notification, called a 'termination notice', must be sent to the DHSS within six months of the employee leaving (unless he is leaving because he has reached state retirement age (65 for a man, 60 for a woman) or has died: in these cases, the DHSS will take the initiative).

The termination notice must be sent to the DHSS, COE Group, Newcastle-upon-Tyne, NE98 1YX. It is the company's legal responsibility to ensure that COE Group are notified, even if the termination notice is completed and sent by the company's pension consultants or insurance company.

All persons having any responsibility for the administration of a pension scheme should acquire a copy of leaflet NP29 which explains how to complete the termination notice, and which type to issue in differing circumstances.

Apart from details of the employee concerned, i.e. his name, National Insurance number and date of leaving, the method of providing for the GMP, together with the method of revaluation, must be given.

15.4.4 *GMP*

The GMP replaces the additional component of State retirement pension forgone because of contracting out and the Widow's Guaranteed Minimum Pension (WGMP) replaces one half of the widow's pension similarly forgone.

In the case of an employee who cannot have more than 20 years' membership of the State scheme after April 1978 and who remains a member of a contracted-out scheme until State pensionable age is reached, there is an exact comparison.

However, in the case of an employee who can exceed 20 years' membership, the additional component is based on the best 20 years' revalued earnings, while the GMP (and WGMP) is calculated without regard to the best 20 years' earnings. A GMP is always calculated from revalued contracted-out earnings factors rather than from actual relevant earnings. Each year a regulation is made called a 'Section 21 order', giving the percentage by which earnings factors are to be revalued.

Should an employee cease to be contracted out (other than by death), then, unless a premium is paid to the State, the GMP accrued to the date of leaving has to be revalued in the future, and unless revaluation is made by reference to Section 21 orders, the GMP and the additional components in respect of contracted-out service will differ.

The DHSS will calculate the additional component in each case as though the employee had not been contracted out and will pay any excess of the additional components over the GMP to the pensioner; the escalation of the GMP and WGMP in course of payment is paid by the DHSS.

15.4.4.1 *Calculation of GMP.* To calculate a GMP, the revalued contracted-out earnings factors (i.e. the employee's earnings in contracted-out employment revalued as in 15.4.6 below) are dealt with in the following manner:

(1) If contracted-out service is less than 20 years, they are multiplied by $1\frac{1}{4}\%$.
(2) If contracted-out service exceeds 20 years, they are multiplied by $\frac{25}{N}\%$ (N being the number of years in the employee's working life, i.e. from age 16 or from 6 April 1978 if he was over 16 on that date, up to State pensionable age (65 for males, 60 for females)).

The result of this calculation is then divided by 52 to give the weekly GMP. Full details of this calculation, with examples, are given in DHSS leaflet NP29.

15.4.4.2 *Calculation of WGMP.* The calculation of a WGMP depends upon the member's status at the date of death, as follows:

(1) If he dies in service, the WGMP is one-half of his GMP calculated as if he had reached State pensionable age at the date of death.
(2) If he leaves and subsequently dies in the tax year of termination (e.g. leaves on 1 October 1982 and dies before 6 April 1983), the WGMP would be calculated as if he had died in service on 1 October 1982 and it should be noted that this WGMP is less than one-half of the GMP calculated on leaving.
(3) If he dies after the GMP is put into payment, the WGMP is one-half of the GMP (including any increase on account of deferred retirement) in payment to the member when he died.
(4) If he leaves and dies after the tax year of termination (e.g. leaves on 1 October 1982 and dies after 5 April 1983), the WGMP would be one-half of the GMP on leaving, revalued for each completed tax year following the year of leaving up to the date of death (e.g. if he leaves on 1 October 1982 and dies on 1 July 1985, the number of years for revaluation purposes would be two).

15.4.5 *Method of providing GMP*

A scheme may provide an individual's GMP by a number of methods:
(1) Preserving the GMP in the scheme, i.e. making the ex-member's pension paid-up, so giving the ex-member a promise to pay it, subject to revaluation (see below) at pensionable age. (Note: the DHSS operate a service by which company pension schemes can trace ex-members when preserved pensions are due for payment.)
(2) 'Buy out' the GMP by purchasing an annuity from an insurance company, the annuity providing the amount of GMP revalued at pensionable age.
(3) Transfer the GMP to another contracted-out scheme that the ex-member has joined.
(4) Pay a Contributions Equivalent Premium (CEP). This may only be paid in respect of an employee ceasing to be contracted out while the scheme continues and when it is not compulsory to preserve a GMP in some other way (i.e., the employee has not had more than five years' contracted-out service or is under age 26).

   The CEP represents the difference between the (lower) contributions which have been paid in respect of a contracted-out member and the full contributions payable in respect of a participating member. An amount equal to the employee's part of the rebated State contributions (the certified amount) may be deducted from any refund of his contributions to the occupational scheme paid to him on leaving. If the difference (or substantially the whole of the difference) has been paid into the occupational scheme, payment of a CEP will not place a strain on the scheme.

15.4.6 *Revaluation of GMP*

As is explained above, during the employee's membership of a contracted-out scheme the GMP can only be revalued in line with Section 21 orders but, should he leave the scheme (other than by death), the accrued GMP may in the future be revalued in one of a number of ways as elected under the scheme. Assuming that the future responsibility for the GMP is not transferred to the State by payment of a CEP but is preserved under the scheme, the accrued GMP must be revalued by one of the following methods:
(1) By Section 21 orders (as it was while the employee was a member of the scheme).
(2) By limited revaluation at 5% per annum with payment of a Limited Revaluation Premium (LRP) to the State in return for the State's providing revaluation in excess of 5% per annum. It should be noted that this method of revaluation is applied by comparing the accrued GMP, revalued at 5% per annum up to and including the tax year before State pension age or earlier death, with the GMP revalued by

Section 21 orders over the same period, and the scheme has to provide the lesser amount as GMP. The important point is that this is an overall comparison, not a year-by-year one.

(3) By fixed revaluation at 8½% per annum (irrespective of the amounts of Section 21 orders). While it seemed unlikely (in early 1982) that Section 21 orders could be less than 8½%, following the reduction in the rate of inflation since that date, it is possible that by selecting this method a scheme could have to provide a larger GMP than it would have had to provide had it elected to use Section 21 orders, because once the 8½% option has been chosen it cannot be changed.

(4) In the event of the withdrawing member joining another contracted-out scheme and a transfer value being paid, the liability for the accrued GMP can be transferred with the member's consent.

15.4.7 *Latest position regarding GMP*

As from 5 April 1983, DHSS regulations permit transfers to be by Section 21 order or at fixed or limited revaluation. This should encourage transfers as the receiving scheme can quantify the GMP liability it is accepting. Alternatively, or if the receiving scheme is not contracted out, the ceding scheme may transfer rights in excess of the GMP only, retaining liability for the accrued GMP (retention must, of course, apply if the receiving scheme is not contracted out).

The only limitations in the new regulations are as follows:

(1) That the 5% or 8½% revaluation rate applying to the transferred GMP cannot thereafter be changed, unless a subsequent transfer is made to a scheme using Section 21 orders.

(2) That the rules of both the ceding scheme and the receiving scheme must permit the schemes to apply the new regulations (most schemes will need to make minor amendments to their rules to do so).

(3) That the regulations can only apply to transfers made after 5 April 1983.

The new regulations also permit schemes to apply the 12% option (see 15.5.1 below) to transferred GMP liabilities which were being revalued by Section 21 orders where a scheme is terminated.

15.5 Cessation of contracting out

15.5.1 *Safeguarding of GMP liabilities*

If a contracted-out scheme is terminated or ceases to be contracted out, provision must be made to safeguard the scheme's accrued GMP liability and the proposals for doing so must be approved by the OPB. SSPA 1975 enables the scheme's GMPs to be calculated, if the employer so chooses, on a fixed revaluation of 12% per annum for the last five years of contracted-out service instead of Section 21 order revaluation for the same period, if this produces a lower liability. Liaison between the OPB and the DHSS (Contracting-Out Employment Group (COEG)) will result in the latter getting in touch with the scheme's administrator to agree the total GMP liability.

15.5.2 *Discharge of accrued GMP liabilities*

The scheme can discharge its GMP liability by purchasing insurance policies, by transferring the liability to another scheme or by paying Accrued Rights Premium (ARP) and Pensioner's Rights Premium (PRP). The ARP and PRP are payable when a scheme ceases to be contracted out and GMPs are not preserved in some form.

ARPs relate to the accrued GMPs of current members and preserved GMPs of ex-members; PRPs relate to those whose GMP (or WGMP) is in payment at the time the scheme ceases to be contracted out.

The State scheme premiums, apart from the Contributions Equivalent Premium (CEP), vary with age and sex and are calculated by the Government Actuary. The assumptions made by the Government Actuary in calculating these premiums are similar to those used in calculating the contracting-out rate. SSPA 1975 lays down an important rule regarding the calculating of these premiums: that the rate of investment return assumed shall not be less than the average increase in the general level of earnings, i.e. a 'negative yield' will never be assumed.

In use these standard tables are adjusted by a Market Level Indicator (MLI) – calculated each month by the DHSS – the purpose of which is to ensure that the premium reflects the current yield on investments and so gives protection against short-term fluctuations in market price.

For ARPs and PRPs, the GMPs on which they are calculated may be determined using a revaluation rate of 12% per annum for each of the past five years before the scheme ceases to be contracted out. The introduction of this 12% figure over five years is really to enable the maximum revaluation liability to be known should a scheme cease to be contracted out within the next five years. In practice, a decision as to whether to adopt the 12% figure would be made having regard to the Section 21 orders in force over the past five years.

If a contracted-out scheme's investments are 'spread' in the same way (or approximately the same) as the model fund, then presumably payment of these premiums should cause no strain upon it. Even if the 'spread' is not close, provided securities are encashable at their market values, the strain could not be a problem and a directly invested fund can be reasonably sure of covering itself should it change to participating in the State scheme. A wholly insured fund, which must depend upon a surrender value to meet these premiums, might not be able to achieve this result.

Appendix 1
Draft investment fund management agreement

THIS AGREEMENT is made the   day

of   BETWEEN   (hereinafter

called 'the Trustee' which expression shall wherever the context so requires or admits include its successor or successors as the trustee or trustees of the Scheme hereunder referred to) of the one part AND
(hereinafter called 'the

Managers') of the other part

WHEREAS:

(1) the Trustee is the present sole trustee of the
Pension Scheme (hereinafter called 'the Scheme') which is administered in accordance with the provisions of a trust deed (hereinafter called 'the Definitive Trust Deed') dated

as amended from time to time

(2) by Clause   of the Definitive Trust Deed the Trustee is empowered to invest the funds of the Scheme in the manner and subject to the conditions of that Clause and by Clause   of the same deed has the right to appoint a manager or managers of all or any part of such funds

(3) the Trustee wishes to appoint the Managers to manage such part of the said funds as is placed in the care of the Managers in accordance with and subject to the terms and conditions hereinafter set out

NOW IT IS HEREBY AGREED as follows:

1.   APPOINTMENT
  (a) The Managers are appointed with effect from
                                as managers of the portfolio, being the cash
      or other investments transferred for the purpose of this Agree-
      ment by the Trustee to the Managers and receipt of which is
      hereby acknowledged by the Managers.
  (b) This appointment supersedes any previous appointment and will
      be for an initial period of one year and thereafter will be termin-
      able by either side at seven days' notice.

2.   DISCRETION
  Subject to the terms of this Agreement and any guidelines given in
  writing by the Trustee to the Managers, the Managers are empowered
  to make purchases and sales of investments constituting the portfolio
  within the general policy agreed at meetings or otherwise with the
  Trustee.

3.   DUTIES OF MANAGERS
  (a) To prepare and supply to the Trustee monthly valuations, and
      quarterly (or at such less frequent intervals as the Trustee shall
      request), progress reports on investments and cash balances
      constituting the portfolio, and to confirm that the Managers have
      made all such transactions entirely within the terms of the
      Agreement.
  (b) To organise and attend meetings with the Trustee at quarterly or
      such less frequent intervals as the Trustee shall request, such
      meetings to discuss reports and valuations and establish general
      lines of investment policy. The Trustee may also request informal
      meetings from time to time.
  (c) Full details of all investment transactions to be submitted daily to
      the Trustee.
  (d) To keep in safe custody all investments, articles, title deeds and
      other documents relating to or in connection with the portfolio.

4.   REGISTRATION
  Investments may be held in the name of a nominee company or
  nominee companies as the Managers see fit on the understanding
  that:
  (a) the Managers will remain directly responsible to the Trustee for
      everything done or omitted by the nominee or nominees as if
      done or omitted by the Managers personally and
  (b) the nominee acknowledges in writing that it holds all such
      securities in its name as trustee for the Trustee.

5. ACCOUNTS
    The Managers will maintain (either themselves or with a Bank approved by the Trustee) fund accounts, to which all investment transactions will be posted. The accounts will itemise, inter alia, investment costs and proceeds, dividends, interest and other income. Cleared balances on bank current accounts are to be transferred daily to (or from) deposit accounts bearing interest at current market rates, leaving only a working balance on current account. Statements of account will be submitted monthly to the Trustee.

6. DEALING
    All transactions within the portfolio will be made on terms at least as good as those which would be available to the Trustee if it were dealing on its own account. The commission charged on each transaction will always be shown on the relevant contract note.

7. FEES
    The Managers shall be entitled to a fee per annum calculated on the following scale:

    per   on the first
    per   on the next
    per   on the balance of the portfolio

    Fees will be paid quarterly in arrear, based on the middle market value of the investment portfolio, excluding any approved 'in-house' investments.

8. LIABILITIES OF MANAGERS
    The Managers will not be liable for investment decisions made in good faith within the agreed policy and the guidelines prepared by the Trustee but will indemnify the Trustee against all loss suffered as a result of the negligence or fraud of the Managers or any of their employees, agents or nominees.

    Signed on behalf of [the Trustee]

                                                              Director

    Signed on behalf of [the Managers]

                                                              Director

Appendix 2
Model layout of a trust deed

Contents list

Parties/preamble – Recitals referring to any earlier schemes and statutory approvals

Definitions (To be inserted here rather than at end of deed)

Appendix 3
Model layout of scheme rules

Contents list

Appendix 4
Computerised monthly membership record statement

PENSION SCHEME

CARD 14206

UPDATE MONTH OCT 1983
RUN DATE 08/12/83
AMENDED 26/05/83

SALARIED SECTION
CURRENT CONTRIBUTOR 51

NATIONAL INSURANCE No.
Branch

SURNAME
INITIALS
AGE 49 YRS 4

SEX MR.
MONTHS

DATES OF

BIRTH	11/06/1934
SERVICE ENTRY	01/06/1960
MEMBERSHIP ENTRY	01/10/1971
ENTRY TO CURRENT	01/10/1971
CLASSIFICATION	
MEMBERS NRD	30/06/1999
PENSIONABLE SERVICE	01/04/1971
RECKONED FROM	
LINKED QUALIFYING	
SERVICE	
DATE OF EXIT	
REASON FOR EXIT	

HISTORY OF EARNING

P-60	PENS	CONTR.	UP TO
9130	7440	37.20	10/83
8660	7120	427.20	09/83
8442	7030	421.80	09/82
6411	5199	312.00	09/81
5928	4914	294.84	09/80
4287	3377	202.68	09/79
4315	3520	211.20	09/78
4110	3418	205.08	09/77
3798	3195	191.76	09/76
2865	2345	140.76	09/75
2259	1733	104.04	09/74
2088	1620	97.20	09/73
2088	1620	97.20	09/72

CONTRIBS 10/71 2742.96 10/83

HISTORY -2ND TIER CONTS

RELEVANT	CONTR.		UP TO
EARNINGS			
7598		474.91	03/83
6996		367.34	03/82
7040		299.24	03/81
5266		210.64	03/80
4237		169.48	03/79

HISTORY OF AVC CONTS

LUMP SUM	ANN AVC	TOTAL AVC	START DATE	UP TO DATE
0	60	5	10/83	10/83
0	60	60	10/82	09/83
0	60	60	10/81	09/82
0	60	60	10/80	09/81
0	60	60	10/79	09/80

CONTRIBS 10/79 245 10/83

PENSION ENTITLEMENTS

	NOV	DEC	JAN
CURPUP	1571.08	1581.00	1590.92
GRSCON	2842.83	2880.03	2917.23
DEATH BENEFIT			27390.00
DEATH IN SERVICE			
DEPENDANTS PENSION			1167.67

SCHEME	RETAINED	MEMBERS	ANNUAL	ESCALATABLE	ADDED
CODE	CONTRIBS	CONTRIBS	PENSION	PENSION	MONTHS
2ORB		62.67			6
TOTAL		62.67			6

STATE PENSION GUARANTEES
1961 GOV GRAD SCHEME 05/04/71
E.P.B. OF 14.70 AT 05/04/1975
RETAINED AMOUNT OF 33.44
1978 STATE SCHEME 06/04/78

MEMBER

GMP AT EXIT
GMP (ACCRUED) 9.96
CEP PAID
CERT AMT

WIDOW
4.98

ESTIMATED RETIREMENT BENEFITS

	MEMBER	DEPENDANT
GPS PENSION	3503.00	1751.50
PAST SERVICE FFB		
PAST SERVICE SLO ESC		
TOTAL PENSION	3503.00	1751.50

Appendix 5
Example of an annual pension benefit statement

IMPORTANT NOTES

1. The calculations overleaf are estimated benefits only. In all cases, a firm quotation will be given immediately prior to retirement, or on leaving service.

2. The Benefit Statement shows the date of joining THIS SCHEME. Any benefits transferred from an earlier scheme have been taken into account.

3. Gross P60 earnings are your total earnings in the tax year ended on 5th April last, BEFORE DEDUCTING Pension Scheme contributions.

4. Pensionable pay is Gross P60 earnings less an amount equal to the State basic pension for a single person.

5. If you have mislaid your Membership Certificate, a duplicate can be obtained on request from your Division Pensions Office.

6. In calculating the Present Expected Pension for a member who is within 5 years of normal retirement date, the pensionable pay is an *average* of the 3 best consecutive years' pensionable pay in the last 10 years, so as to give a more accurate indication of the final anticipated entitlement.

7. Widow's and dependant's pensions are normally payable for life, except that:
   a) A widow's pension is subject to review on remarriage, and
   b) A pension to an infant dependant will cease at age 18, or on completion of full-time education if later.

8. Further information on the benefits of the Scheme is contained in the Explanatory Booklet in which your entitlements on leaving service are described.

9. In any correspondence with the Department of Health and Social Security concerning your benefits under this Scheme, your National Insurance Number, and the 'ECON' and 'SCON' shown on the front of this Benefit Statement, should be quoted.

THIS STATEMENT HAS BEEN ISSUED BY:

ANY QUERIES SHOULD BE ADDRESSED TO YOUR DIVISION PENSIONS OFFICE

ANNUAL PENSION BENEFIT STATEMENT AS AT OCTOBER [83]

Name: [MR] [JT] [   ]   National Insurance Number [   ]

Division Pension Office: [ABC]   Branch Reference: [   ]

This Statement shows the benefits available to you and your dependants under this Scheme.
IT SHOULD BE READ IN CONJUNCTION WITH YOUR MEMBERSHIP CERTIFICATE.
It is based on the following information:

Date of birth	11/06/1934	
Date of joining the company	01/06/1960	
Date of joining this Scheme	01/10/1971	See note 2
Normal retirement date	30/06/1999	
Gross P60 earnings for year ending at last 5th April	9130	See note 3
Pensionable (Gross P60 earnings less 'Disregard')	7440	See note 4

1. PRESENT EXPECTED PENSION AT NORMAL RETIREMENT DATE
If you remain with the company until normal retirement date you will receive – based on your pensionable pay of [7440] – a pension of

[3503.00] p.a.

This is equivalent to [47.80] % of pensionable pay, or [38.37] % of gross P60 earnings.

On your death after retirement a pension of [1751.50] p.a. would be payable to your widow or dependant (see note 6).

2. LEAVING THE SERVICE OF THE COMPANY
If you had left the service of the company in October [1983] you would have

been entitled to a deferred pension of [1559.92] p.a. starting at

normal retirement date, or an equivalent transfer payment to the scheme of a new employer. Refunds of contributions on leaving are now restricted by law (see note 7). FOR INFORMATION, your total contributions paid up to the above date were

[2805.63] plus additional voluntary contributions of [245.00]

3. DEATH IN SERVICE

If you had died in October [1983] a lump sum would have been payable to your

dependants, of [27390.00]

In addition, if you had left a widow or dependant,

a pension of [1167.67] p.a. would have been payable (see note 6).

Appendix 6
Example summary of principal actuarial assumptions used in valuation

Demographic assumptions

Rates of mortality, retirement and withdrawal from service have been adopted which have been found appropriate for similar schemes in the public sector. All members who have not left service prior to attaining age 60 (or age 65 in the case of male members) have been assumed to retire at that age.

Each male member is assumed to be married, at retirement or in the event of death in service, to a wife who is on average three years younger than her husband. It has been assumed that female members will receive a return of their family benefit contributions (if any) on termination of membership.

Rate of interest

A valuation rate of interest of 8% per annum has been adopted. This represents the rate of interest expected to be earned on the existing assets and on the investment of all future contributions to the Scheme over the long-term future, covering the period until all the present members have retired and all benefits arising from their membership have been paid, i.e. a period of 80 years or more.

Salary increases

Provision has been made for increases due to age, merit, seniority and promotion by the adoption of a salary scale which has been found appropriate following an investigation of the progression of the average salaries from age to age of the members as at the valuation date in quinquennial age groups.

Provision has also been made for increases in the general level of salaries of 7% per annum. Investment earnings on the Fund in excess of the assumed rate of 8% per annum will be available to offset the cost of salary increases in excess of the assumed rates.

Pensions increases

Increases awarded up to and including the awards on 1st October 1981 and 1st December 1981 have been allowed for in the valuation. Provision has been made for future increases in pensions of 4% per annum. Investment earnings on the Fund in excess of the assumed rate of 8% per annum will be available to offset the cost of pensions increases in excess of the assumed rate.

Assets of the Fund

The Market Value of the Quoted and Unquoted Investments (other than Property) on the valuation date was adjusted to the average level of market values during the three-year period ending on the valuation date, and credit has been taken for this adjusted Market Value in our valuation. The part of the Property portfolio which was revalued as at 30th September 1981 was included at the values certified by the retained surveyors to the Fund as at that date, while the remainder of the Property portfolio together with the Net Current Assets, have been included at the amounts shown in the Accounts.

Appendix 7
Example of a form of pension application for transfer and entry into a merged pension scheme

FORM OF AGREEMENT ON JOINING

GROUP PENSION SCHEME.

In connection with the provision of new benefits under the Payroll Staff Section of
the   Group Pension Scheme (the Group Pension Scheme).
FROM:
NAME IN FULL
PRIVATE ADDRESS

DEPARTMENT
COMPANY

TO:
1.   LIMITED
2.   PENSION TRUST LIMITED (The Trustees of the Group
                     Pension Scheme)
3.   LIMITED (The Company)
4.   PENSIONS No.1 LIMITED ⎱ Trustees of the
                                              ⎰   Limited
5.   PENSIONS No.2 LIMITED ⎰ Employee Pension Scheme
6. The Committee of Management of the   Limited Employee Pension
   Scheme (The Committee)

WHEREAS

I have read the attached Explanatory Rule Booklet of the Group Pension Scheme and the Announcement Leaflet.

NOW IN CONSIDERATION OF

My admission to the Group Pension Scheme on 1st April, 1974 and the provision for me thereunder of the benefits described in the said Booklet.

I AGREE

(1)   That the assets representing the accrued benefits secured under the rules of the   Employee Pension Scheme shall be transferred to the Trustees of the Group Pension Scheme.

(2)   In consequence thereof, I hereby release the Trustees and the Committee of the   Employee Pension Scheme in respect of such transferred assets.

(3)   I authorise the Trustees and the Committee of the   Employee Pension Scheme to make any changes in the Trust Deed or Rules of that scheme which may be required to put the above transfer into effect.

AND

(4)   That contributions at the rate of 4% can be deducted by my Employer from my pay.

To be returned to your Personnel Manager
for onward transmission to the Group Pensions Officer

SIGNED:

DATE:

Checked

SIGNATURE:

IMPORTANT NOTE See reverse for notice of Company's intention to apply for election as a contracted out employment.

Appendix 8
Model set of accounts

Model Income and Expenditure Account for the year ended 31st December, 1982

	1982 (£'000)	(£'000)	1981 (£'000)	(£'000)
Contributions for the year				
Normal – Members	520		430	
– Company	937		770	
Special	46		34	
Voluntary	51		46	
Transfer values from other schemes	11	1,565	6	1,286
Benefits for the year				
Pensions to retired members/ dependants	315		238	
Lump sums on retirement	132		93	
Lump sum death benefits	57		51	
Contribution refunds to members leaving service	44		79	
Transfer values to other schemes	12		5	
Payments to the state pension scheme	27	587	41	509
Contributions less benefits		978		777
Income from investments				
Dividends/interest from Stock Exchange securities	384		294	
Rents from properties	113		106	
Interest from short-term investments	124	621	98	498
Money available for investment		1,599		1,275

Model Balance Sheet as at 31st December, 1982

	1982 (£'000)	(£'000)	1981 (£'000)	(£'000)
Fund at 31st December 1981		5,835		5,207
Money available for investment	1,599		1,275	
Profits/(losses) on sale of investments	176		(67)	
Unrealised appreciation/(depreciation) in market values of investments during the year	2,122	3,897	(580)	628
Fund at 31 December 1982		9,732		5,835
Represented by:				
Fixed interest securities	1,341		829	
Equities and convertibles	4,198		2,163	
Short term loans and deposits	1,176		300	
Freehold property	2,260		2,095	
Insurance policies	780		830	
Cash	109	9,864	22	5,939
Money due to the Fund (e.g. income due but not yet received, tax recoverable and outstanding contributions)	108		97	
Less Money due by the Fund (e.g. refunds, transfer values, pensions and death benefits awaiting payment)	(240)	(132)	(201)	(104)
		9,732		5,835

Appendix 9
Useful addresses and telephone numbers

Association of Consulting
  Actuaries
Rolls House, 7 Rolls Building
London EC4A 1NH
Tel: 01–831 7130

Association of Pensioneer Trustees
Somers House, Linkfield Corner
Redhill, Surrey RH1 1BB

Department of Health and Social
  Security
Alexander Fleming House
Elephant and Castle
London SE1 6BY
Tel: 01–407 5522

Department of Employment
8 St James's Square
London SW1
Tel: 01–214 8695

Department of the Environment
Tolworth Tower
Surbiton, Surrey KT6 7EA
Tel: 01–399 5191

Faculty of Actuaries
23 St Andrew Square
Edinburgh EH2 1AQ
Tel: 031–556 6791

Government Actuary's
  Department
22 Kingsway, London WC2B 6LE
Tel: 01–242 6828

Institute of Actuaries
Staple Inn Hall, High Holborn
London WC1V 7QJ
Tel: 01–242 0106

The National Association of
  Pension Funds
Sunley House, Bedford Park
Croydon CRO 0XF
Tel: 01–681 2017

Occupational Pensions Advisory
  Service
Room 327, Civil Aviation House
129 Kingsway, London WC2B 6NN
Tel: 01–405 6922 ext. 205

Occupational Pensions Board
Lynwood Road, Thames Ditton
Surrey KT7 0DP
Tel: 01–398 4242

The Pensions Management
   Institute
PMI House, 124 Middlesex Street
London E1 7HY
Tel: 01–247 1452

Pensions Research Accountants
   Group (PRAG)
c/o MPA, Metropolitan House
Northgate, Chichester
Sussex PO19 1BE

The Society of Pension Consultants
Ludgate House, Ludgate Circus
London EC4A 2AB
Tel: 01–353 1688

Superannuation Funds Office
   (Inland Revenue)
Lynwood Road, Thames Ditton
Surrey KT7 0DP
Tel: 01–398 4242

Glossary of pension terms

This Glossary contains definitions of the main terms used in pension fund administration. Where terms used in a definition are themselves defined elsewhere in the Glossary they appear in italics.

Accounting standard
A Statement of Standard Accounting Practice (SSAP) issued by the Accounting Standards Committee (ASC) of the major UK accounting bodies.

Accrual rate
The fraction of the final pension earned for each year of pensionable service, e.g. 1/60 or 1/80 of final pensionable salary.

Accrued rights premium (ARP)
A premium payable to the State scheme when a scheme ceases to be contracted out and no other arrangements have been made to guarantee the *Guaranteed Minimum Pension* benefits for a member below State pensionable age.

Actuarial assumptions
The assumed rates of interest, wages and pensions inflation, the movement of retail prices and the mortality rates applied by the *actuary* to the valuation of a pension scheme.

Actuary
A member of the Institute of Actuaries or the Faculty of Actuaries (Scotland) who is recognised by the *Occupational Pensions Board* for the purpose of providing Certificates of Solvency under SSPA 1975 and is professionally qualified to make valuations of pension schemes.

Added years
A credit of additional years of pensionable service in his new scheme which may be given to an incoming member in consideration of the *transfer value* payment made by his previous scheme, or following a merger, in respect of his previous pensionable service.

Additional component
A phrase used to describe upper tier earnings under SSPA 1975.

Additional Voluntary Contributions (AVCs)
Contributions made by the member to build up additional pension benefits to the Inland Revenue limits of 15% of total earnings, after all ordinary annual contributions to the pension scheme have been taken into account. The overall limit on total pension benefits at NRD will also apply to both ordinary and *additional voluntary contributions*.

Administrator
A person having the management of a scheme for the purposes of FA 1970 s.26(1).

Annuity
A regular fixed payment made at periodic intervals for life in return for a capital sum.

Approved scheme
A scheme granted approval by the *Superannuation Funds Office* under the provisions of FA 1970, Part II, Chapter II.

Augmentation
An increase of pension entitlement over and above the normal scheme pension scale which may be granted during service or in deferment or while on pension.

Average salary scheme
A scheme in which the benefits are related to the level or grade of salary during each specified period of pensionable service.

Basic component
The flat rate State pension equivalent to the single person's State pension under the State scheme arrangements. (SSPA 1975, s.6(1) refers.)

Capital gains tax
A tax imposed on the capital profit realised on the scale of any chargeable asset after offsetting any capital losses. It is subject to certain statutory exemptions and indexation.

Capital transfer tax
A tax payable on all transfers of personal and real property during lifetime or at death subject to any statutory exemptions, e.g. between spouses and above the accumulative limit of £64,000 (1984).

Centralised scheme
This can refer either to a group scheme serving a number of companies within the same financial group or to an industry scheme serving several companies not necessarily with financial links.

Certified amount
That part of the *Contributions Equivalent Premium* which can be recovered out of any refund of scheme contributions to a member.

Closed scheme
A scheme which is closed to new members but which otherwise functions as a normal pension scheme for its continuing members and pensioners.

Commutation
The exchange of the whole or part of a pension entitlement for a tax free lump sum at the time a pension is due to come into payment.

Concentration of investment
A term used by the *Occupational Pensions Board* to denote a degree of funding, generally in excess of 10%, in any single investment in a pension fund portfolio.

Contracted in
A term often applied to a scheme which is not contracted out of the earnings-related part of the State scheme.

Contracted-out employment
Refers to membership of a scheme which has contracted out of the earnings-related part of the State scheme coverning the *additional component* in return for which a lower rate of contribution is payable to the State scheme.

Contributions
This covers normal annual, special and additional contributions. An employer must make contributions to secure SFO approval of a scheme to which employees may or may not contribute.

Contributions Equivalent Premium (CEP)
A premium which is payable to the State scheme when a contracted-out employer wishes to transfer to the State scheme the liability for the GMP entitlement of an employee who is leaving service after a relatively short period of employment. It is equivalent to the rebate allowed on the State scheme contributions for a contracted-out employee and his employer.

Controlled funding
A funding plan in which an insurance company determines the required rate of contribution for a fund by reference to the overall liabilities of the scheme.

Controlling director
As defined in ICTA 1970 s.224(1). Until 1970 such a director was not permitted to join an *occupational pension scheme*.

Corporate trustee
A limited company incorporated under the Companies Acts which acts as the trustee to a pension scheme, provided the necessary powers of appointment are contained in the trust deed.

Deferred pensioner
A member who has withdrawn from service and for whom a preserved benefit is payable to him or his dependants from a future date.

Dependant
A person who has been wholly or partially financially dependent upon the deceased member or pensioner at or near to the time of his death or his retirement.

Deposit administration
A form of funding offered by life offices for *insured schemes*.

Discontinuance valuation
One of the forms of valuation adopted by the *actuary* to determine the degree of

solvency and the extent to which all accrued liabilities are covered in the event of the scheme terminating at the date of valuation.

Discretionary scheme
A type of scheme for which admission and the rate of contribution are entirely at the discretion of the employer who will normally bear the whole cost of the scheme.

Dynamism
A word used to denote *escalation* or *indexation* of a pension in deferment or payment.

Endowment assurance
A form of insurance which provides a lump sum at maturity or earlier death in return for a premium payment. It can be with or without profits.

Equal access
It is one of the basic requirements of SSPA 1975 for all schemes that the same eligibility requirements should apply to both sexes for entrance to the scheme, whether or not they wish to contract out.

Escalation
Another word used to denote the regular increase of a pension in payment or deferment.

Exempt approved schemes
A scheme approved under FA 1970 which laid down new criteria (the New Code) for the approval of *occupational pension schemes* and became mandatory for all schemes after April 1980.

Final average remuneration/earnings
This refers to the actual method of calculating *final pensionable salary* which can vary but must still come within the permitted Revenue limits.

Final pensionable salary
The formula adopted by the individual scheme for determining the salary to be applied to the accrual rate and calculating the amount of pension entitlement. Sometimes it is the actual rate of salary in the final year, but the average of the three best years in the last ten can give a more equitable result for employees with variable earnings.

Final salary scheme
One in which the pension benefit *accrual rate* is related to the actual salary in payment at or near the time of retirement or at the date of leaving service.

Fixed rate revaluation
This is when a fixed rate of *escalation* (currently $8\frac{1}{2}$% per annum), as opposed to a variable rate, e.g. the Retail Price Index, is applied to the GMP in deferment.

Franking
When scheme rules permit, the additional cost of revaluing a GMP during deferment can be offset against the balance of the scheme pension entitlement at NRD. After 1984 it is likely to be prohibited.

Funding
An actuarial method used to determine the rate of contribution required to maintain the scheme's assets and liabilities in balance taking one year with another.

Graduated pension scheme
The 1961 State graduated pension scheme (the Boyd-Carpenter scheme) which covered a limited range of earnings above the basic State pension level for the period between 1961 and 1975.

Guaranteed Minimum Pension (GMP)
The minimum benefit requirement for earnings in the band between the *upper* and *lower earnings limits* for a member of a contracted-out scheme.

Hancock annuity
An immediate *annuity* for a former employee, the cost of which is allowed as a business expense in the year of payment. It can relate either to an annuity where no company pension is payable or to the *augmentation* of the scheme pension.

Income and Corporation Taxes Act 1970 Section 226 policies
This Act laid down the basis for determining the permitted pension benefits for self employed persons or those not in a company scheme.

Indexation or inflation proofing
A form of *escalation* of pension benefits either before or during payment related to the movement in the Retail Price Index.

Insured scheme
A pension scheme covered by means of a policy with a life office for which premiums are paid in return for which the pension benefits due are guaranteed.

Integration
An allowance made for State scheme benefits in the benefit structure of an *occupational pension scheme*, irrespective of whether it is contracted in or out. This can be arranged either by adjusting the pensionable salary or the final pension entitlement.

Interim trust deed
An interim deed covering the formation of an *occupational pension scheme* which will enable the SFO to give their provisional approval and permit contributions to be treated as allowable expenses and the normal tax relief allowed on investment income until the definitive deed is submitted.

Limited revaluation premium (LRP)
A premium payable to the State scheme when a member leaves service and his GMP is to be subject to revaluation geared to *Section 21 orders* but limited to a maximum of 5% per annum.

Linked qualifying service
Periods of service in one or more schemes covered by transfer credits which are aggregated with current scheme service to determine the length of pensionable service for preservation requirements.

Long service benefits
This refers to the pension benefits payable under SSA 1973 to a member at *normal retirement age* in his scheme, which may not be the same as the State pension age.

Lower earnings limit
Under the SSPA 1975 the State scheme covers all weekly gross income between the *upper* and *lower earnings limits* the latter of which is approximately equivalent to the basic State pension for the single person.

Managed fund
A pension fund which is managed by a life office for which units are issued as opposed to the general aggregated pension fund. It can also be treated as an ordinary portfolio investment.

Mixed benefits
A term used in the SFO *Practice Notes* when the benefits available to a member on leaving service are composed partly of a refund of contributions and partly of benefits in some other form such as a deferred pension.

Money purchase scheme
A scheme by which the benefits earned each year are purchased each year for each member and the contributions adjusted thereby in relation to each member's actual pensionable earnings in that year.

Net relevant earnings
Under ICTA 1970, s.226 these are the maximum annual earnings after any allowable deductions on which personal pension policy contributions may be based.

New Code
FA 1970 laid down the revised conditions of the Inland Revenue for the approval of *occupational pension schemes* in Part II, Chapter II and these became compulsory for all schemes after April 1980.

Non-participating employment
Under the 1961 Boyd-Carpenter scheme an *occupational pension scheme* was allowed to be non-participating in the State scheme for the additional earnings component if that were provided by the private scheme.

Normal retirement age
The age laid down for retirement on full pension in the scheme rules. It need not necessarily be the same as the State pension retirement age but it must be approved by the SFO.

Occupational Pensions Board (OPB)
Part of the Joint Office (OPB/SFO) set up under SSA 1973 with statutory responsibilities for overseeing the management of *occupational pension schemes*.

Occupational pension scheme
A scheme which is capable of recognition as a retirement benefits scheme under Part II, Chapter II of FA 1970.

Old Code
The classification of Revenue approval for *occupational pension schemes* prior to 1970. All Old Code schemes should have amended their trust deed and rules so as to comply with FA 1970 by April 1980.

Ordinary annual contributions
Contributions by the employer and the members of an *exempt approved occupa-*

tional pension scheme on a regular basis which are allowed for tax relief in the year of payment.

Pay As You Go scheme
A non-funded arrangement whereby pensions are paid out of revenue by the employer.

Pension
A form of *annuity* payable by the trustees of an *exempt approved scheme*. It may be guaranteed for five years irrespective of the date of death.

Pensionable earnings
Those earnings which qualify for the calculation of pension benefits and in respect of which contributions are paid. It is still common for overtime and special types of pay to be excluded.

Pensioneer trustee
The SFO require an independent pensioneer trustee to be appointed to all small self-administered Section 226 schemes.

Pensioner's rights premium (PRP)
A payment made to the State scheme when a scheme ceases to be contracted out, in return for which the State scheme will take over the GMP liability of any scheme member or pensioner over State pensionable age.

Practice Notes
Originally an unofficial document issued by the SFO setting out the manner in which they exercised their discretionary powers under FA 1970 regarding pension schemes. It was reissued by the OPB in 1979 in Joint Office publication IR 12/79, but is still referred to as the 'Practice Notes'.

Preservation
All FA 1970 approved schemes are required to include in their rules provision for the preservation of accrued pension benefits for pensionable service in excess of five years for all members aged 26 or over when a refund of contributions is no longer permissible.

Qualifying service
A term defined in SSA 1973 and used to refer to pensionable service in an approved scheme for which pension benefits have to be preserved for service over five years.

Relevant benefits
These refer to the pension and lump sum cash benefits which are provided under the schemes for which SFO approval has been granted. It does not refer to any benefits arising from disability or death by accident during service. (FA 1970 s.26(1) refers.)

Requisite benefits
The scale of benefits for the member and his legal widow to be provided under the scheme rules before contracting-out approval can be given under SSPA 1975.

Retirement annuity contracts
This is generally taken to refer to a s.226 scheme for self-employed persons.

Section 21 orders
These lay down the annual revaluation factors to be applied to the GMP both in payment and while deferred, unless a *limited revaluation premium* or a *fixed rate* basis has been chosen in lieu.

Section 32 arrangements
Under FA 1981, s.32 a scheme member, on withdrawal, can if the rules permit ask that his transfer payment is made to purchase a life *annuity* in his own name.

Section 226
Self-employed pension arrangements under ICTA 1970 for persons not in any *occupational pension scheme.*

Self-administered scheme
A pension scheme in which contributions are invested other than by means of an insured contract through an external or in-house fund manager and controlled by the trustees.

Self-invested scheme
A scheme which has the whole or a substantial part of its assets invested in the employer company. It would be difficult to envisage the OPB granting contract-ing-out approval to such a scheme.

Short service benefits
The benefits to which a member is entitled on withdrawal from service before *normal retirement age* under the *preservation* requirements of SSA 1973.

Solvency tests
These form part of the tests applied to determine the adequacy of the funding to provide the benefits promised and they are used to substantiate the actuarial certificates required by the OPB for contracted-out schemes.

Special contributions
Any contribution other than normal or additional contributions, payable nor-mally by the employer either as a single lump sum or by instalments spread over a limited number of years.

State scheme premium
The *Contributions Equivalent Premium* which is payable to the State scheme to cover the transfer of the GMP on withdrawal from service if it is not retained in the member's scheme.

Superannuation Funds Office (SFO)
A branch of the Inland Revenue responsible for the administration and approval of *occupational pension schemes.* Now located with the Occupational Pensions Board in the Joint Office.

Transfer value
The cash sum which is payable by the scheme trustees in accordance with the rules for the transfer of a member's benefits to another scheme on withdrawal from service.

Transferability
The facility to take a *transfer value* payment for pension benefits and pay it over to another scheme in return for a benefit credit in that scheme of either added years or a paid-up pension.

Upper earnings limit

The weekly limit of gross earnings adjusted annually up to which earnings-related contributions are paid to the State scheme and in excess of which no further benefits accrue. Approximately equivalent to a figure seven times the amount of the *lower earnings limit*.

Upper band earnings

Earnings which fall between the *upper* and *lower earnings limits*.

Vested rights

Any accrued pension benefits to which a member would be immediately entitled on withdrawal from service or at retirement.

Waiting period

That preliminary period after the commencement of employment before an employee becomes eligible for membership of a pension scheme.

Index

References to numbered paragraphs in the text, not page numbers, have been given throughout this index.